The Christian's Guide to Money Matters for Women

The
Christian's Guide
to
Money Matters
for Women

Mary Lynne McDonald
Certified Financial Planner (CFP)

ZondervanPublishingHouse
Grand Rapids, Michigan

A Division of HarperCollinsPublishers

The Christian's Guide to Money Matters for Women
Copyright © 1995 by Mary Lynne McDonald

Requests for information should be addressed to:
    Zondervan Publishing House
    Grand Rapids, Michigan 49530

Library of Congress Cataloging-in-Publication Data

McDonald, Mary Lynne. The Christian's guide to money matters for women / Mary Lynne
    McDonald.
       p.   cm.
   ISBN: 0-310-50160-1
   1. Women—Finance, Personal.   2. Finance, Personal—Religious aspects—Christianity.
  I. Title of Book.
  HG179.M3744   1995
  332.024'042—dc20   95-10010
                                                                       CIP

All Scripture quotations, unless otherwise indicated, are taken from the *Holy Bible: New International Version*®. NIV®. Copyright © 1973, 1978, 1984 by International Bible Society. Used by permission of Zondervan Publishing House. All rights reserved.

Edited by Mary McCormick
Interior design by Sherri L. Hoffman

Printed in the United States of America

95 96 97 98 99 00 / ❖ DH / 10 9 8 7 6 5 4 3 2

*This book is dedicated to the countless women I have met,
counseled, consoled, advised, and advocated for
over the years. Their stories have touched my heart and
stirred me to action. May God bless each of you as you
carry on with faith and perseverance.*

❧

Contents

ACKNOWLEDGMENTS

To my husband, Mike, for trusting God with everything we have ever done. Thank you always for believing in me and for being the spiritual giant you are.

To God, whose patience with me was an essential ingredient of this project. Thanks, Lord, for always being there.

INTRODUCTION

This book was written from my heart....

The purpose of this book is to help women understand money in very practical and commonsense ways. It is written to teach the basic skills of money management, investments, and financial planning, and how to make good financial decisions, as well as how to cope in an emergency. Why do women need to learn these skills? Because:

- Approximately 50 percent of all women will be divorced at some time in their lives, left to face the family finances on their own, and
- Since women outlive men, 80 percent of all married women will be widowed and will, sooner or later, be faced with the responsibility of handling money alone.

Too often, however, women are unprepared for this task because they and their husbands have assumed that money management and investments should be handled by men.

I have heard many women say when the subject of money management comes up, "He understands business better than I do," and "I was never taught anything about money," or "I wouldn't know the first place to start." They just assume that men are better at handling money management and business than women are, but this is often NOT the case. And, considering that sooner or later most women will be alone, either from divorce or widowhood, learning to handle money is just very good common sense.

Take the example of Millie, who was married for twenty-eight years to a fine man who handled all financial decisions. He had assured her that "everything was taken care of," meaning that she should not worry or concern herself about their finances.

Millie took her husband at his word, but at age fifty-four he unexpectedly died of a sudden, massive heart attack. Millie was absolutely devastated! She could not cope with the many important decisions that had to be made, and she needed a great deal of help to find out where she stood financially.

She discovered, to her dismay, that this fine man had left her with only twelve thousand dollars worth of life insurance, no pension, thirteen years left on a mortgage that she thought had been paid off, a business debt that was now due (as a result of his death) and payable to his business partner, and a bunch of speculative penny stocks of questionable value. She had absolutely no idea where to begin! She had bills due and no income. She was in a crisis, and she was really scared!

This sad story is replayed over and over again, every day, all across America. Women have neglected to become educated and, when suddenly divorced or widowed, find out that they are in really bad financial condition, with limited solutions, little knowledge, and no confidence. They are easy prey for the unscrupulous, and they generally make poor financial decisions that they deeply regret later.

An example of a case like this that comes to mind is a young widow with three children still at home who asked me what to do with the twenty-five thousand dollars of life insurance she had just received from the death of her husband. I recommended that she put it in a money market fund for six to twelve months and start keeping a record of her expenses so that we could work out a budget for her. Without working, she would have no income, but her children would each get Social Security until they reached eighteen. The youngest was fourteen, and she felt certain that the money that the children would receive would be enough for the family to live on.

Problems started when a family member came to her and suggested that she invest the money in a piece of land, convincing her that she would make more money this way than with a money market fund, which was only paying 7 percent interest at the time. She invested fifteen thousand dollars in the real estate.

Then, because she was under stress and experiencing a lot of grief, she succumbed to the need to shop and ended up impulsively buying new carpeting for her home. That cost her about three thousand dollars. She spent the remaining seven thousand dollars of insurance money on car repairs, clothing, luxuries for her children (because she felt guilty), and a vacation for all.

This woman was ill-equipped for her new job as financial decision maker, had no experience in investments, and knew nothing about her living expenses when all of this happened. The Social Security income proved inadequate to live on and stopped a few years later. The real estate was illiquid and could not be sold at the time that she needed money for living expenses. The carpeting was nice but added little to the value of the home, and she felt stupid for having bought it. She had made three bad decisions and ended up selling her home one and a half years later to solve her financial problems.

I counsel with countless women and hear their stories at conferences, classes, and on talk shows. I hear them tell me how they let their husbands "handle the money" and when these husbands died or left, how lost they were, not only at being left alone but also at making financial decisions, paying bills, handling savings and investments, and budgeting their income.

I have listened to these and other women tell me how much they wish that they and their husbands had shared the financial burdens more, how much better it would have been if they had simply known what he was doing, how much income he made, how it had to be spent, where he had invested and *why,* and what provisions had been made for her in the event of his death. Their cry was to be involved and informed—a small issue with a GIANT impact.

I work with numerous women going through divorce. These women frequently come to me, afraid and panicked. Too many have never written checks or balanced a checking account, have no idea how to budget, have no cash to get started, and no experience in making financial decisions. Their husbands earned the money, spent the money, made all of the financial decisions, controlled all of the assets, and had all of the experience with money management for the family. These women are like sheep walking directly into the mouths of hungry wolves. They will become financially consumed and destroyed by their lack of knowledge and experience.

When I started out by saying that this book was written from the heart, I had in mind all of the women whom I have counseled over the years, all of the women who have attended my classes and seminars, all of the women whom I have talked with casually or professionally, and all of the women who will ever read this book. Most will be widowed, many will be divorced. All will benefit by *knowing how to handle money now—before the crisis occurs.* Most can prevent the pain of being left helpless—by taking steps *now* to become financially knowledgeable and capable.

If this is your hope as well, then this book was written for *you.*

An Overview of Concepts

*I*f you are reading this book, the chances are good that you already believe that you need to learn the principles of financial planning.

However, just to provide you with a basic understanding of why it is scriptural as well as profitable to learn how to manage money, save, invest, and plan your finances, I would like to begin with a look at the scriptural basis for financial planning.

Scripture has a great deal to say about money. There are over nine hundred references to money in the Bible—more even than to heaven or hell, which indicates that God appears to be very concerned about the issue of money, doesn't He? Is this because He needs money . . . or considers it evil . . . or is there some other reason?

Obviously, God does not need money. He already owns all of it. What you have is only yours temporarily, in your keeping and control as a steward on His behalf. And He does not consider money evil, either. It is not money itself that is evil; it is the *love* of money that is evil. Money is *neutral!*

The reason that the Bible talks so much about money is that God knows even if you do not know, and especially if your world does not know, that your attitude about money reflects the condition of your heart in many ways. God is very interested in the condition of your heart, hence, He is very interested in your attitudes; and your attitude about money is a clear reflection of your relationship to Him.

Money itself is neutral, neither good nor bad by itself. How you react to and with money can be either good or bad, however. If money becomes so important to you that you give it more attention than you give to God, or if money causes you so much anxiety and stress that it succeeds in pulling you away from God, money has then perverted or subverted your relationship with God. Material possessions, which are purchased or obtained through money, have the same potential power and represent the same danger to your spiritual well-being because they can pull you away from God as surely as can money by itself.

God is concerned about money, then, because it is a barometer of your spiritual condition. If you are greedy, He can easily know that by how you handle (or hoard) money. If you are careless with money (and waste or spend it foolishly), He can easily know that by how you handle money also. And so on. God can easily gauge our spiritual condition by looking at the ways in which we use, abuse, handle, waste, keep, invest, save, spend, and give money.

Christians, as well as secular people, need to learn how to use money effectively and efficiently without letting it become an idol or a burden beyond their bearing. When you have plenty of money, or receive an excess, your plenty or your excess can be either a blessing or a burden. Anyone who has never had money and suddenly finds himself or herself with a lot of it can tell you, Christian or not, that the responsibilities, the decisions, and the stresses of dealing with that money are sometimes more than they imagine, sometimes more than they can bear. This is how money can pull you away from the Lord.

The purpose of this book is to educate women about the practical management of money and help them to avoid the traps that money sets for all of us, in accord with the timeless truths found in Scripture. As a married woman, you are, among other things, a "helpmeet" to your husband, jointly responsible for the financial integrity of your family. As a single woman, you are even more responsible; you are responsible for ALL of the financial integrity of your family. In either case, once you understand how to manage money and have a good money management system in place, you will have your finances under control, and they will be in the proper place in your home. Money will not control you or your family, it will not be the cause of stress or anxiety, it will not become a deterrent to your faith. Your first resource for making good financial decisions should be Scripture. This book is intended to give you the practical knowledge to implement the wisdom you will find in Scripture.

2 WHERE DO YOU START?

Naturally, *the best place to start is at the beginning.* That is with Scripture. Begin by reading all that the Bible has to say about money.

There is much of this wisdom in Proverbs, but search your concordance and other research helps for mention of money and material possessions in other places of the Bible as well. Pray about the verses you read. Ask God to teach you His truths, particularly about money and material things so that you can become a wise and careful steward. At the end of this book is a chronological listing of Scriptures that deal with money, which may help you. When you are done, you will have the best and most applicable set of guidelines ever written on how to handle money. This book will serve only as a practical addition to that set of scriptural guidelines.

CAUTION: Do not take only one Scripture, or use a Scripture out of context, as your entire set of guidelines in making financial decisions. Do not base all of your understanding about money on one passage of Scripture. Take *ALL* of the Scriptures in context and in their entirety when searching for the wisdom and guidance that they provide.

HOW CAN YOU KNOW HOW TO HANDLE THE DETAILS?

The Bible is clear about money and material possessions, but it does not go into very much detail. It will NOT tell you which bank you should use for your savings and checking accounts, or which specific appliance to purchase, or which investment is right for you or your family, or the best method of investing for retirement. *That is up to you to decide and do, using biblical principals to guide you.*

This book, from here on, will teach you the practical details, the "worldly information" . . . so to speak . . . *that will equip you in making detailed financial decisions as you learn about money and prove yourself a good steward.*

After reading the Scriptures that deal with money, you will want to begin on a practical basis to understand and use money wisely. *The first step is to take action by identifying your concerns and problems with money,* discussed next. This will enable you to set some good financial goals, which is the practical beginning for all who are serious about getting a handle on their money. *So, on to STEP #1!*

STEP #1: IDENTIFYING PROBLEMS AND GOALS

You are probably concerned about something if you are reading this book and are willing to become educated about money. Before you try to apply the methods outlined in this book, you first need to make a list of your concerns, your financial problems, and your goals. Notice that I do not say "financial goals" but just "goals." That is because your overall goals will, in fact, depend on your financial problems being under control and solved. It is all part of a bigger picture.

Some of your goals will be specific, such as "start a savings plan" or "get out of debt." Others will be somewhat vague, such as "maintain my standard of living" or "have enough money to support our family." *Your goals will be unique, so spend some time writing them down.*

Below is a very typical list of the kinds of goals and concerns or problems that I have seen in my years as a professional financial advisor:

- Save money for emergencies
- Get out of debt
- Have a comfortable lifestyle at retirement
- Live within a budget
- Plan and choose good investments
- Build up a nest egg for the future

- Buy a home
- Be able to afford to travel
- Be able to afford private school for children
- Maintain our standard of living
- Keep up with or do better than inflation in the cost of things we buy
- Save or invest a specific amount of money monthly
- Accumulate a certain dollar amount of money by a certain date
- Solve our financial problems
- Use credit wisely

Whatever *your* goals and concerns, *list them* as clearly as possible. As you progress through these chapters, they will gradually become more specific. Go back and redefine them as this happens. As you read and think about what you are reading, if you realize that you have a financial problem or goal that you had not realized before, go back and add it to your list. *This process will take some time but is very worthwhile. Stick with it, and it will eventually pay some good rewards.*

A Special Note to Christian Women:

To my dismay, I have found that women—Christian women in particular—are woefully ignorant about money, financial planning, retirement planning, business planning, investments, taxes, and estate planning. Recent surveys indicate that as few as 20 percent of American women know much of *anything* about their family or personal finances, could not cope in a financial emergency, have no idea of how much income the family will have at retirement, where that retirement income will come from, what to do in the event of the death or disability of their husband or self, how many assets the family has, where the money is saved and invested, what is involved in probate at death, whether or not the breadwinner carries adequate amounts of life insurance, and where to turn for help in a financial emergency.

This is a clear indication that women, and especially Christian women, have neglected to assume any responsibility for the financial welfare of their families, leaving it entirely to the men, even if those same women hold down jobs and earn wages.

Because most women will be widowed and half will be divorced, some at an early age, this sad state of affairs is a sure invitation to trouble—trouble that *could be avoided with good planning.* I do *not* advocate that women *specifically* take over the handling of the family finances, especially if they and their husbands have decided that the husband will do this, but I DO advocate that women be completely aware of every financial detail in their family and BE ABLE to take over if and when it becomes necessary, *as it most likely will.* In some cases, the couple will decide that the wife *will* handle the family finances, probably because the couple has concluded that God has given her the greater skills and talents to do so. But this should be a point on which both agree. It should not be a matter to divide the couple.

In those cases where the husband is irresponsible and does not handle money well but refuses to allow his wife to assist and advise him, I advise that the couple pray sincerely for help and seek counseling. Not doing so will eventually result in serious financial and marital problems that could have been avoided if each partner in the marriage had been willing to submit to the counsel and help of the other, which includes financial counsel and advice.

NOTE: One of the biggest areas of financial problems comes from being self-employed or the owner(s) of a small business. Routinely, I have found that self-employed people and small-business owners have serious financial problems that have a negative impact on the marriage and the family, due largely to some specific and avoidable reasons. The last chapter of this book deals with those financial problems and the reasons they occur. If you or your husband are self-employed, or own a small business, please take time to reread that chapter carefully.

STEP #2: IDENTIFY PROBLEMS

To solve a problem, you have to identify it first. This means that you will need to "see the enemy" if you want to have victory over the enemy.

If your problem is that you cannot pay all of your bills each month, say so. If your problem is that you worry all of the time about money matters, say so. List all of the problems, even if they do not translate into a specific financial or material lack or need. Things that concern you, even though you are not presently experiencing financial difficulties, should be listed also because concerns can and often do turn into real problems through anxiety or worry.

STEP #3: TAKE A PICTURE OF YOUR SITUATION

This means to find out where you are today with your finances. It is like having a starting point in planning a trip. You need to know where you are before you start out on a trip, in order to wind up where you want to go. Otherwise, you will, instead, end up going around and around in circles. You will get lost, or take a long, costly detour. With your finances just as with anything else, *you need to know where you are before you start out.*

So, How Do You "Take a Financial Picture" of Your Situation?

You do this by completing the financial data forms shown next in this book. The first is called a "Net Worth Statement." *Don't let the title scare you off! Don't skip this!* You cannot reach your goals of being a good steward and meeting the long-term financial needs of yourself and your family if you skip this step. *And, it is not as hard as it sounds.* This information will tell you:

- whether or not you owe more than you own
- how much progress you are making each year on your finances
- if your spending is under control or out of control

Here is an example of a net worth statement. Start by filling in the blanks. If you do not know the answers, ask whoever *does* know until you complete this for yourself. If you have to call banks, or credit card companies, or mortgage companies, or anywhere else, do so. *Begin today* to find out what you own and what you owe. *Complete this net worth statement, and be on your way to financial integrity.*

Next, complete the "Cash Flow Statement." From this, you will find out if you have too many bills or debts and where the money is going. This information found in the cash flow statement will help you in setting up a realistic budget, one that will actually work, rather than one you idealistically come up with and then totally ignore after a month because it cannot work. It will also help you to calculate how much life insurance to carry on the breadwinner if the breadwinner were to die suddenly. Below is an example of a typical cash flow statement (sometimes called "income and expense statement"):

NET WORTH STATEMENT

ASSETS

Cash _____

Bank Accounts:

Checking _____

Savings _____

Certificates of Deposit _____

Stocks/Bonds _____

Mutual Funds _____

Annuities _____

Pension Plans:

401-K _____

Profit-Sharing _____

Stock Bonus Plan_____

Deferred Comp Plan_____

403(b) Plan _____

Others_____

SEP Plan_____

IRA–husband _____

IRA–wife _____

Investment Real Estate _____

Life Ins. CASH VALUE_____

Business Value _____

Life Insurance loan(s) _____

Home Value_____

Other (specify)_____

Other _____

TOTAL ASSETS:_____

DEBTS

Home: 1st mortgage_____

_____

Home: 2nd mortgage _____

Home equity loans(s) _____

Investment RE loan(s) _____

Vehicle loans _____

_____

Credit Cards_____

_____

_____

_____

Department Stores _____

_____

Bank loan(s)_____

_____

Finance Company loan(s)_____

_____

Relatives loan(s)_____

Credit Union loan(s) _____

_____

Business loans _____

_____

_____

TOTAL DEBTS: _____

   TOTAL ASSETS:_____

– **TOTAL DEBTS:** _____

= **NET WORTH OF** _____

CASH FLOW STATEMENT

INCOME	PER MONTH	PER YEAR
Wages (take-home)	_____	_____
Husband	_____	_____
Wife	_____	_____
Bonus	_____	_____
Alimony	_____	_____
Child Support	_____	_____
Social Security	_____	_____
Pension Income	_____	_____
Rental Income	_____	_____
Interest Income	_____	_____
Dividend Income	_____	_____
Real Estate Contracts	_____	_____
Trust Income	_____	_____
Other Income	_____	_____
TOTAL INCOME	_____	_____

EXPENSES (Remember that some are *not* monthly but are quarterly or annually):

	PER MONTH	PER QUARTER	PER YEAR
Tithe	_____	_____	_____
Savings	_____	_____	_____
Mortgage	_____	_____	_____
Rent	_____	_____	_____
RE Taxes	_____	_____	_____
Child Support	_____	_____	_____
Alimony	_____	_____	_____
Retirement Plan	_____	_____	_____
Contributions	_____	_____	_____
College Costs	_____	_____	_____
Groceries	_____	_____	_____
Utilities (all)	_____	_____	_____
Car payment(s)	_____	_____	_____

Credit Card(s) _____ _____ _____

Department Store(s) _____ _____ _____

Bank Loan(s) _____ _____ _____

Personal Loan(s) _____ _____ _____

Car Insurance Premium _____ _____ _____

Health Insurance Premium _____ _____ _____

Life Insurance Premium _____ _____ _____

Homeowner Insurance _____ _____ _____

Other Insurance Premiums _____ _____ _____

Private School _____ _____ _____

Student Loan(s) _____ _____ _____

Clothing (cash) _____ _____ _____

Child Care _____ _____ _____

Subscriptions _____ _____ _____

Uninsured Medical
    /Dental _____ _____ _____

Personal Care _____ _____ _____

Clubs _____ _____ _____

Sports _____ _____ _____

Recreation _____ _____ _____

Travel _____ _____ _____

Gifts _____ _____ _____

Christmas _____ _____ _____

Restaurants _____ _____ _____

Entertainment _____ _____ _____

Back Income Taxes _____ _____ _____

Other (specify) _____ _____ _____

TOTAL _____ _____ _____

TOTAL INCOME

– TOTAL EXPENSE

= EXCESS _____ _____ _____
    or SHORTAGE

Now, after this exercise in bookkeeping, do you see whether or not your expenses exceed your income? If so, in what areas could you spend less? In the calculation for your net worth, did you find out that you owe more than you own? Why do you believe this is so? If you do not owe more than you own, how much is your *net* worth? Has it gone up or down over the last few years? In either case, do you know why?

Getting these exercises down on paper, then getting the answers to the questions that they raise, is the beginning of getting your finances under control. *You will not get out of debt or reach any financial goals by chance; you can and you must calculate your net worth and your cash flow. Everything follows those two things.*

3
ANALYZING
FINANCIAL PROBLEMS

Since you have just finished your net worth and cash flow statements, you now have the tools, the "picture" needed to analyze why your financial problems exist and to try some solutions to get rid of them. Your next step is to look at these tools (net worth statement and cash flow statement) to learn the root of the problem.

Look first at your net worth. Is it a positive or a negative amount?

If it is negative, this means that you owe more than you own. If you had to sell everything, you would wind up in the red, in debt. And this is bad. Why? Because at some point in your life, you will no longer be able to work for income, no longer be able to borrow money. What if the Lord called you into a mission field that required that you sell everything and GO? If you could not pay off all of your bills with the proceeds of the sale of your possessions, you would not be able to obey the call to go, would you? This is financial bondage.

Is your home a debt? That depends on several things. First, do you owe more on it than you could get, after selling costs and real estate commissions, if you sold it? If so, it represents a debt. However, if you sold your home and netted more than you owe on it, it does not represent a debt. Instead, it is an asset. These days, few people can pay cash for a home; most have to get a mortgage. The Bible does not say that you cannot borrow; it cautions that the borrower is the servant to the lender. The reason for this caution is to warn believers that the result of debt can be bondage, servitude, slavery. Your credit cards and department store credit accounts are the easiest and most common ways for you to get into this kind of bondage. More on these topics later.

So, reviewing your net worth statement shows whether or not you are in overall debt even if you are able to pay your bills presently. If you manage your money well, your net worth should grow larger each year. This is NOT hoarding money, as some might claim. Your net worth needs to increase each year merely to keep pace with inflation, for one, and so that you will have enough available at retirement on which to live when you stop working for a wage. It is not hoarding to store up enough (did you catch that word *enough?*) on which to live when you can no longer work. It IS hoarding if you consistently try to accumulate more than you need or refuse to spend what you have accumulated for normal expenses. It IS hoarding if you have an excess and refuse to give of it. It IS hoarding if you are so afraid of losing some of it that you refuse to take reasonable investment risk with your money. It is NOT hoarding to anticipate how much you will need to live a normal life at retirement, or to anticipate the cost of an upcoming expense, or to anticipate how much savings you need to see you through an emergency, or to anticipate the cost of a college education for your children or grandchildren, and to then attempt to accumulate that much for those purposes.

Now that I have driven home that point, let's take a look at the next step in analyzing your financial problems. To do this we need to now look at the cash flow statement you completed. This statement tells you how much income and how much outgo you have. If your outgo exceeds your income, you have a cash flow problem called "not enough money" or "too many bills." In other words, you are spending more than you are earning. The results of this kind of life are that sooner or later you will be in debt, usually deep debt. It also frequently means that you will have to sell your possessions to pay off bills. You end up gradually "spending your net worth." Ultimately, you wind up at retirement with no assets and no income because you have spent all of the assets on bills and earn no income due to retirement. On what will you live now?

Obviously, if you are reading this book, you should not end up in this terrible condition, but many, many Americans *do*. The average net worth in America, the land of plenty, one of the richest nations on earth, is only about six thousand dollars total. Yes, after all is added up and subtracted, after figuring out what is owed from what is owned, the monetary value of the average American's entire lifetime of working is only six thousand dollars! Why is this so?

Usually, it is because of poor money management habits, lack of skills, ignorance about money matters, or from fear or greed. Fear and greed may surprise you; I will explain that later. First, let's look at poor money management as a reason for the dismal financial condition of most Americans today.

POOR MONEY MANAGEMENT

This usually involves chronic overspending. It is the direct result of "impulse buying" or buying everything on credit, or buying "without a plan." Is this a problem in your household? If so, take close note of the solution to this problem:

DO NOT SPEND ANYTHING over a set, predetermined amount without a ten-day "cooling off" period. During this ten-day cooling-off period, ask yourself the following questions:

1. Do I really need this item?
2. Will I be glad next year that I have this item?
3. Why do I want this item so badly?
4. Will anyone benefit from this item? Who?
5. If I buy this item, will I have to give up something else? What?
6. How important is the other item I will give up? Why?
7. Can I afford to buy this item with cash?
8. Can I afford to save money to buy this item later?
9. How long will it take to save the money to buy this item later?
10. Would it be better if I waited to buy this item later with cash?

If you honestly like the answers that you give yourself, buy the item in question. You will find, however, that oftentimes you will talk yourself out of the purchase and feel really great about it! When you do, this means that you are learning restraint and discipline—really good habits and attitudes to have.

PROBLEM AREA #1: LACK OF SKILLS   •

LACK OF SKILLS is simply the result of not being taught how to manage your money. This usually shows up in a checkbook that never balances (you do balance your checkbook every month, don't you?); bills that you charge and forget are coming due until you get the bill; failure to save regularly; overspending on items that you need, such as cars, refrigerators, houses, and so forth when you could have paid less; poorly chosen investments; chronic late payments on bills that should be paid on time and could be with a budget and spending plan; purchases that you didn't really need are ultimately unsatisfying because they add to your burden of debt in some manner.

LACK OF SKILLS usually involves some degree of ignorance about financial matters. This does not mean that you are an ignorant person; it simply means that you have not learned yet what you need to know. Almost everyone is capable of learning what she needs to know about money, once the information is given to her. Women, I have found, are often extremely capable, even if they have never had any prior training or experience with money. I think that this stems from the natural ability that many have in dealing effectively with details. Handling money involves LOTS of details, to be sure, like record keeping, budgets, and taxes. Women, including homemaking women, deal all day long with endless details, sometimes minor ones, that repeat themselves day after day. This is excellent training for managing money.

PROBLEM AREA #2: IGNORANCE ABOUT MONEY

IGNORANCE ABOUT MONEY is usually the result of not having the opportunity to handle money, or of complacency about money, or maybe the result of being very poor early in life, or being taught that money is dirty or bad all by itself, thus to be avoided at all costs, and sometimes is the result of just plain laziness. When any of these is the case, that individual just avoids ever learning anything about money or never has the opportunity to learn anything (increasingly rare these days). In addition, many husbands tell their wives "not to worry about it: I have taken care of it" and, in effect, keep their wives totally ignorant of the financial affairs of the family for as long as the husband is alive. Statistically, most wives will outlive their husbands and find themselves completely overwhelmed with money decisions and questions exactly at a time when they are least capable of learning anything. This is a real shame, especially since most of these husbands have not, in fact, "taken care of everything" as they claimed to have done. If this is your situation, start now to determine that you will become knowledgeable and wise about your family's money matters.

PROBLEM AREA #3: FEAR AND GREED

FEAR AND GREED are major contributors to the terrible financial condition in which most Americans find themselves after working all of their lives and finally retiring. Why do I say that?—because fear is usually one side of an evil coin, with greed the other side. You will need to think about this carefully to understand what I am saying here, and you will need to pray earnestly about it if you suspect this affects you.

Fear involves the emotion of being afraid of something. When I speak of this kind of fear, I am not referring to healthy fear, such as fear of grizzly bears, or the reverent fear that is part of being in awe of God. These are good kinds of fear, because they keep us out of trouble. I am talking about ungodly and unhealthy fear—the kind that cripples people, stops them from making a financial decision because they are afraid that it will be the wrong decision. I am talking about fear of investing or saving money because you do not want to risk losing any of it.

In my financial planning practice I have counseled thousands of clients, Christian and non-Christian, who are unable to take any action to solve their financial problems, solely because they are afraid to do something.

These people are unable to correct a problem, such as too much debt, because they are afraid to change their lifestyle now. They are afraid to save money for an emergency because they have heard that a lot of banks might fail, and they are afraid of losing their savings in the bank if this happens. They are afraid to invest in mutual funds because mutual funds are not guaranteed, and they fear that the stock market will collapse again.

I tell these people that indeed these disasters may occur. They have already occurred, many times in history. Wars and other calamities will also occur, but we have to go ahead with our plans anyway. As Christians, we have the assurance that God will provide for us as He sees fit—not necessarily according to *our* plan, of course, but always providing us with what we need. Sometimes, despite the best investment, or the safest bank, or the most cautious plan, we will lose money. My intuition is that sometimes this is God's plan for us, that it is sometimes the best thing that could happen to us.

Our job in managing money is to become wise and not be foolish, not to dissipate or waste the money that we have been given. It is also our job to trust God to do what is best for us even if things turn out badly for us in our financial affairs.

This means that in addition to trying very diligently to become really good stewards, we have to learn to trust God. In addition, we must become trustworthy ourselves. It is not a one-way deal; it is a two-way deal—between us and God together. This requires that we make good and sensible financial decisions.

I have heard Christians, and sometimes non-Christians, say that it is "wrong to be concerned with money, to save, to invest, or accumulate any money beyond what we need today." This is like saying that it is wrong to plan. However, Proverbs directly contradicts this! People who say this generally base their viewpoint on a nonmaterialistic position, or on the Scripture where Jesus tells His followers not to worry about today, not to be concerned about what they wear or eat. However, Jesus was not telling His followers not to plan, to be lazy, to give up working for a living and wait for money to fall from heaven into their laps. Nor was He telling them that it was unimportant to Him that they were clothed and fed. He was telling them that they should not WORRY . . . and that is a far cry from not working, not saving, not planning, not investing for reasonable future expenses. The key is in *not worrying,* rather than in planning and saving up.

Earlier I warned the reader not to take isolated Scriptures out of context on which to make financial decisions. Christians who claim that it is up to God entirely to provide for them, that it is wrong to plan or save or invest, are indeed taking Scripture out of context and basing their positions on isolated

Scriptures. To handle money responsibly within the godly guidelines given in the Bible, you must take all of Scripture in total and in context.

PROBLEM AREA #4: BUDGETING

Another area of major problems for many people is the family budget. Too many people claim that "a budget doesn't work," or is "too much trouble," or is "impractical." What they are really saying is that they don't want to bother with it.

You will, however, initially need a budget if you want to solve cash flow or net worth problems. There is no other way around this issue. If you spend too much, you will need to use a budget to track down all of your spending. If you are gradually spending down your net worth, meaning cashing in or selling assets without replacing them with other assets, you will have to use your budget to track down where this money is going each time you sell an asset.

This requires a budget—it is as simple as that. Don't cringe and get sick at the thought of a budget! If you do, consider using the term *spending plan* instead. To many people, this is more appealing, like calling your diet an "eating plan." And, this is truly what a budget is: a plan on how to spend your money . . . a spending plan.

Did you ever think about what you can actually *do* with money? You can invest it, you can give it away, you can save it, you can spend it . . . and that's *all* you can do with it.

You cannot eat money, or wear it, or drive it, or live in it, or stay warm with it, or learn anything by looking at it, or confer wisdom with it. You cannot buy friendship or love with it, either, as some people try to do, and you and I both know that those who do are sadly mistaken about money.

Whether or not you buy them now or later, through savings and investments, money can only be used to buy *things*. That is the purpose of having it. If you do not spend it now, you can only save or invest it, or give it away. In light of these choices facing you, you might as well have a plan for what you want to do with your money and learn how to do it wisely.

So, in thinking about what you can and cannot do with money you will, hopefully, arrive at the conclusion that to handle it properly, you will need a spending plan or budget.

Before you jump into your own budget, however, let me share with you my experience to illustrate why some budgets don't work and are doomed to failure (sort of like why some diets do not work). Some budgets fail because:

- they are based on false data (you "fudged" on the figures)
- they are too restrictive (like a starvation diet)
- you ignore them once they are written down (they were just academic)
- you cheat
- you are too deep in debt

If you have tried to budget before, or have never tried because you are sure you will fail, or have never tried because you absolutely hate the thought of a budget, reconsider the idea now, thinking of it instead as a spending plan. A detailed budget concept is presented in chapter 5, which you can use to set up your own budget.

Get Started Now

The sooner you have a good budget and use it (you do have to use it), the sooner you will become a good and wise steward with your financial problems on the way to being solved. Your budget will have to be flexible but not so much so that you can easily violate it every month. By "flexible," I mean that it cannot be rigid and unyielding, denying your family truly necessary care, such as medical treatment. However, if you delay any monetary decisions to spend for at least ten days, pray about them before committing yourself to the purchase, educate yourself as much as humanly possible about the facts in your specific financial situation, seek wisdom from Scripture and good counselors, follow biblical guidelines, and trust God with every penny, He will provide even in the most impossible situations. This includes helping you with a budget problem that you encounter and cannot solve. This is why your budget must be flexible instead of rigid, to allow God to work His will instead of the budget's always bending to your will.

PROBLEM AREA #5: RISKS

Other problems that you may have and frequently overlook if you are average, are the risks that you face every day and can plan for. Notice that I said, "plan for." There are many risks that you cannot plan for and will have to learn to let go of—to trust God about—such as wars, or worldwide economic disasters, bank failures, investment losses, and lawsuits.

Most risks can be insured against, however. This is indeed wisdom and prudence to do so. Again, I have heard some folks, including Christians, say that if you buy insurance, you do not trust God. How silly!

God gave us the good common sense to prepare against disaster and the specific instruction to plan for trouble by anticipating it and taking action to offset it. This sounds as though God had insurance in mind, to be sure. Why do I say that? Because this is exactly what insurance is intended to do—offset a possible disaster by anticipating it and taking action through the insurance policy to cover the risk.

Too many people complain about the cost of insurance. They are exhibiting a degree of greed when they do. Never, never, never have I heard anyone complain when their insurance paid off when a house burned down, or a car was wrecked, or the breadwinner died. People only complain when things are okay and the premiums have to be paid. That is greed! I am not, mind you, implying that all insurance policies are equally priced, or that you should not be careful how much you pay in premiums. I simply mean that there will be a cost, and not to recognize that the cost is necessary is a form of greed.

What Risks Do You Face?

The most devastating, in all respects, is death. When a breadwinner dies, the entire family is hurt beyond description. The grief is unspeakable. The emotional pain is impossible to avoid, but Christians, at least, have the Lord to comfort them at this time.

However, without good financial planning, the financial impact of death can be almost as hurtful as the emotional. I have provided some examples next from true cases that I have witnessed in my own financial planning practice. The names have been changed to provide privacy to the women in these examples, but these are all true cases.

EXAMPLES AND SOLUTIONS

EXAMPLE #1: CAROL

Carol is now forty-three, the mother of two teenagers. Her husband, Jim, was killed in an auto accident two years ago. Jim was forty-two at the time of his death. He had been employed as a pipefitter for the government; Carol and Jim lived a traditional life; she was a homemaker and he was the breadwinner. They were very involved in their local church and had been married for eighteen years at the time of Jim's death.

Carol knew absolutely nothing about the family finances. Jim had been a good provider and took care of all of the finances. He paid all of the bills every month and made all of the financial decisions. Carol never asked any questions about money except to inquire whether or not they could afford some item that she felt that they needed.

At Jim's death, Carol was shocked to find out that they owned no life insurance on Jim. It was a difficult task for her to determine this, as she did not know where Jim kept the financial papers in their home. She had to search through a stack of paperwork in his desk and became very frustrated, discouraged, and fearful in this process. Most of what she found made no sense at all to her, and she came to me, nearly hysterical with worry and "information overload." I found that Jim and Carol had made no wills, so Carol would be forced to go through the court-ordered probate process, at some expense. In addition, without any life insurance, she would not have access to enough cash. There was less than six hundred dollars in their joint checking account, and only $385 in their savings account. Jim's paycheck had stopped, and there were bills to pay. Carol had no idea what bills they owed, how to pay them, how to balance the checkbook to see whether or not the account balance shown in the checkbook was correct, and whom to contact to ask questions.

Carol and I determined that Jim had been in a pension plan through his job, but unfortunately, most of the benefit would not be available to Carol until she would be age fifty-five, thirteen years away—a lifetime for Carol. She was near to panic by this time. However, we also found that Jim had been saving money through his paycheck, through a payroll deduction, and had $14,500 in this payroll-savings plan. This money was immediately available to Carol, once she was able to supply his employer with the proof of Jim's death and their marriage. Because Jim and Carol resided in a community-property state, Carol was his beneficiary without question. Had they resided in a non-community-property state, she might not have had that assurance. Remember, they had no wills; without which, state laws regarding death will prevail.

Ultimately, we also discovered that Jim had been covered for death in a group life-insurance policy that his employer provided. It would pay Carol thirty-four thousand dollars in death benefits. Now she would have a grand total of $49,485 on which to live . . . for the rest of her life. Since Jim had been earning $34,000 per year in salary, Carol soon realized that this amount of money was not going to last very long.

Indeed, it lasted less than eighteen months. To get Jim's estate settled, Carol had funeral expenses, legal fees, court costs, and my own fees to pay. By the time all of that was done, she had enough money to live only one year. After that, her only choices were to either go back to work or sell their family home. However, I calculated for her that if she did sell the family home, the net profit would only be about sixteen thousand dollars and would last just six to eight months.

In all, Carol faced losing her home only two years after losing her husband. Her children had lost their father, and now were losing all that was familiar to them, all that provided their sense of security in the time of their greatest emotional need. On top of that, their mother was a basket case, frazzled and overwhelmed with money worries at a time when she should have been a comfort and support to her children.

Because her children were under age sixteen, Carol was entitled to Social Security survivor benefits and with this income has been able to keep her family together while she works out a plan to survive long-term. These benefits will end when each child turns eighteen, but they are providing a bare minimum on which to survive while Carol gets training to be able to work at a paying job. *Be aware,* however, that unless you have minor children, you will *not* get widow's or survivor's benefits from Social Security *prior to age sixty* (unless you are disabled) regardless of how great your need. Many women, probably most, are not aware of this "age sixty black-out rule."

Now, two years later, Carol has begun school and will qualify for a job that will enable her to support herself and her family. She has been able to keep the family home, but only because Jim's parents have helped her financially by making the house payments for her. Carol plans to pay them back. She will be in school for one year and will return to work as a registered nurse after a seventeen-year absence from the nursing profession. The chances are moderate to good that she will get a job at a small, local community hospital, but this is not guaranteed. The pay, if she does get the job, will be enough for her to live comfortably, at least as long as she is working.

Retirement is a big concern, however, because the pension that Jim had, which Carol will get someday, will be very small. Jim had only been in that pension for twelve years and had not accumulated very much in retirement benefits, and of course, there were no further contributions after his death. Carol is going to have to save and invest every month out of her own paycheck, and also contribute to Social Security, to be able to expect a reasonable and modest retirement. She has learned all about money, the hard way, and has proven to be a very good financial manager. She is continuing to learn every day. Carol would have preferred, however, that her education about financial matters had come long before the tragic death of her husband. Every widow I know would agree with that statement.

EXAMPLE #2: DORIS

Doris is sixty-one years old. Her husband, Dave, died last year at the age of sixty-seven after a long battle with cancer. The illness took all of the nurturing skills that Doris could muster, and she felt that she had no time or energy for anything else; rightly so, perhaps, considering her situation. You see, Doris had never had any responsibilities or any role in the financial affairs of her family. Dave had, like Jim in Example #1, taken care of all of the finances.

Doris came to me in a panic. She had found my business card stapled to some financial papers in Dave's desk. He had come to me the year before his death to get some investment advice on a mutual fund that he owned. After giving him the investment advice he sought, I had recommended that he see his CPA for some tax answers regarding capital gains if he sold the mutual fund. I also recommended that he have a new will, with a trust drawn up to distribute his estate to his wife and settle it at his death. Dave had, it turned out, seen his CPA for tax advice but had never gotten around to the meeting with the attorney. He died without ever updating his will or setting up a trust for his wife.

Doris was flabbergasted to learn that Dave left her an estate worth several million dollars! She had no idea that she now owned so much. Sounds good, you say? Not necessarily, dear reader. Continue reading. Most of their wealth was in real estate, and some of it was for sale, with a potential buyer on one of the bigger properties. Doris was overwhelmed and totally incapable of making a wise decision about this matter. She was not even aware that, along with her husband, she had signed the real-estate listing with the realtor who was handling the sale of the properties that were listed.

In working with Doris, I learned that the income from the real estate (from rents) was going into a bank account that Doris had not signed on and did not even know existed. It was not too complex to change the account from Dave's name to her name, but even this little detail was quite trying and confusing to Doris. She had to learn, and was very unhappy that she would be required to repeat this process about thirty-five times over the next few weeks, on the paperwork connected with the other assets they owned.

Gradually, with my help and that of the family attorney and the counselor that I convinced Doris to begin seeing, she got the title to all of the family assets changed over to her name, and the probate process proceeded normally. It took eleven months to complete the settlement of the estate. Although no federal or state inheritance taxes were due, Doris spent almost sixty-five thousand dollars on legal and professional fees. Doris will have her own will written, with trust included, to be assured that her estate will now pass to her six children without an estate tax that I estimated at almost one million dollars on her real estate assets, given a normal life-expectancy for Doris and modest appreciation of the value of the properties.

The result of all of this is that Doris is being forced to make critical business and financial decisions that she is not equipped to make on her own. Without expert professional guidance, she would already have fallen prey to any number of financial schemes. For instance, she was approached by a relative who wanted her to sell her home and the real estate and reinvest in a condo in Hawaii. It was, of course, supposed to be a really "good deal"; they always are. The family member was the agent on the condo and would make a substantial commission on the sale, of course. There is nothing wrong with that; on the contrary, the commission is legal and customary. What was wrong was being approached at all at such a time in her life, and the pressure that was put on Doris at a time when she could not make that kind of decision. Her attorney and I advised her to do nothing for a year, and we then met to discuss her options.

To pay her legal expenses, Doris was forced to sell a piece of real estate at a time when real estate prices were low. In the following year, the value of the property that she had been forced to sell shot up by 37 percent, according to her tax assessment. Doris had obviously sold at exactly the wrong time, because her husband had forced her to by not encouraging and facilitating her understanding of the family finances. Prior to coming to my office for advice, she also sold the stocks and mutual funds that he had accumulated on the poor, inexpert advice of a family member who fancied himself something of an investment guru. These, too, were sold at a bad price. Since then, the market has gone up, and those stocks and mutual funds are worth 58 percent more than when she sold them. Doris panicked and made some bad financial decisions, succumbing to pressure and bad advice from her family, because she was afraid that she had no money on which to live—because she was totally ignorant of the family finances.

The saddest result of all of this for Doris is not financial want; she will not live in poverty, or have to find a job to survive. The saddest result is her growing anger at her deceased husband for leaving her alone and vulnerable to deal with all of these things that are so foreign and troublesome to her. She will need extensive counseling from her pastor and a professional therapist to be able to forgive her husband. She complains bitterly that he had always told her "not to worry because everything was taken care of"—and that turned out not to be true!

These examples only illustrate how important it is for a woman to understand where her family stands financially. They are not meant to condemn or criticize these husbands. I could tell you additional stories of women whose husbands did not die but left and no longer supported their family financially. I could tell you about women whose husbands did not die and did not leave home but who became disabled through an accident or an illness that made them unable to work. I could tell you of women who were in abusive relationships, suffering from violence in their homes, who left their homes just to be safe. All of them needed to know how to handle money, each for a different reason and from a different perspective. None were prepared to make financial decisions, handle money, explain to attorneys and judges what their financial situation was, or anticipate and communicate the needs of themselves and their families. *Most were simply unprepared for financial responsibility.*

Most of these husbands had done the best they knew how to do, but they did less than necessary, and their wives allowed it. Most men tell me that they would be *happy and relieved* to know that their wives were capable and willing to take over all or part of the family finances, especially in a necessity. Too many wives simply ignore the issue and load down their husbands with one hundred percent of this burden.

Happily, most women can learn all that they need to know about money and finances. The basics are not that difficult to learn. Most women can and should discuss regularly with their husbands the status of the family finances and offer advice or suggestions from time to time. Even if the husband does not die prior to the wife, even if he does not become disabled, or leave due to divorce, the woman should help him with the finances. Single women have no choice, of course, and should always be well-informed and ready to make good financial decisions.

OTHER RISKS BESIDES THE DEATH OF THE BREADWINNER

There are risks other than the death of the breadwinner that you should know about. Most of them can be avoided or reduced if you know about them ahead of time and prepare for them. Proverbs warns us that an unwise man (or woman) sees danger ahead and fails to prepare for it. As a wise steward, we can avoid this mistake. What are these other risks then? They are listed below:

1. DISABILITY: When this happens, who will produce the income that the family needs? How will medical and physical therapy, if needed, be paid for? How will your family's goals and dreams be achieved (they usually require money)? Who will make the financial decisions?

2. MEDICAL CATASTROPHE: Who will pay the three hundred thousand dollars in organ transplant costs, or months of intensive care in a hospital and institution? Will life-saving medical procedures be available if you cannot pay for these?

3. MAJOR UNPLANNED EXPENSES: How will you pay for nursing-home costs if one of your parents, or a disabled spouse, or a child, goes into a nursing home? How will you be able to afford to replace the aging car or large appliances that you have that are falling apart?

4. UNEMPLOYMENT: How long can you pay your monthly bills if the breadwinner becomes unemployed? Would you have to contact your creditors to explain why you could not pay the Sears bill, or the electric bill, or the doctor bill? How long would it take you to catch up after the breadwinner went back to work? Do you have any savings to protect you in this event? How much?

5. LIABILITY: What would you do if someone fell on your porch and injured himself, then sued you? Where would you come up with two hundred fifty thousand dollars (or millions) in damages awarded by the court if you were found at fault? How would you pay the attorney?

SOLUTION#1: INSURANCE

Fortunately, most of these risks can be avoided or reduced with insurance. That is what insurance is for. It is *not* a savings plan, or a retirement plan, or a college-funding plan. It is a *"risk management plan,"* a way to manage the risks you face and could not otherwise pay for if one or more of these things actually happened. You simply pay the premium (the payment due), and the insurance company takes the risk for you. It is no longer *your* risk. Your premium cost represents only a small fraction of the cost in any one of these kinds of claims. *Insurance is a cheap way to protect yourself against risks.*

FOR EXAMPLE, if someone fell on your porch and sued you for two hundred fifty thousand dollars, and it was covered by your homeowner's insurance, which is not unusual, your three hundred dollars per year of homeowner's insurance premium that you have paid for the last ten years would amount to about 1 percent of the actual cost of this claim against you ($300 x 10 years = $3000—$3000 ÷ $250,000 = 1.2%).

Of course, if you have no claims, you cannot calculate what a bargain this insurance was, but if you ever do have a claim, your insurance suddenly becomes very valuable and very much a bargain! As I stated earlier, I have never heard anyone complain about the insurance benefits that get paid when they have a claim, especially a large claim—only about the cost of the premiums paid before a claim is filed.

Good financial planning and good money management requires that everyone carry adequate amounts of insurance, of all different kinds, to cover these kinds of risks. Failure to do so is flirting with danger and bad stewardship.

HOW MUCH LIFE INSURANCE IS ADEQUATE? Young families should insure the life of the breadwinner for about eight to twelve times *annual expenses*. This means that if it takes $2,500 per month to run your household and meet your routine monthly expenses that the breadwinner should be insured for $240,000 to $360,000. The calculation is:

$2,500 x 12 = $30,000 x 8 = $240,000 or $2,500 x 12 = $30,000 x 12 = $360,000.

For a discussion about the various kinds of life insurance and which is best for you at a specific age, please study the details of this subject in chapter 7.

WHAT ABOUT DISABILITY INSURANCE? Disability insurance is the solution to loss of income if the breadwinner becomes disabled for any reason. This can and does happen to young people, not just to older people. In fact, statistically, it happens more frequently to the under-forty-five-year-olds than the over-forty-fives. And, certain kinds of jobs have a higher risk of disability, as do certain kinds of personalities. If you or your husband is a bus driver, or a firefighter, or a logger, or a fisherman, or in law enforcement, or in one of several other hazardous kinds of work, disability is a very real danger. If you or your spouse is a worrier, eats poorly, lacks a healthy lifestyle including adequate rest or exercise, or is what is commonly referred to today as a "stress junkie," disability from heart attacks or stroke, especially after age forty, is a very real risk you face. And once your spouse becomes disabled, he may never be the same, including his ability to earn an income even if he does not die from his accident or illness. Disability can, in fact, be as financially bad as if death had occurred and is a serious risk for any couple. Disability insurance is the solution to this risk.

Disability insurance is sometimes available from the employer and is usually pretty inexpensive if purchased in this way. Some people in hazardous occupations, however, just cannot buy disability insurance. If this is your situation, be aware of this risk and make other plans to cope in the event of a disability.

If you *can* buy disability insurance, it will pay a continuing "salary" to the disabled breadwinner, the insured, usually about 60–70 percent of the actual wages that would have been earned. Disability benefits are generally only paid for a certain, specific period of time, depending on the policy purchased, and often are tax-free. Some policies pay for five years, while others pay until retirement at age sixty-five. Some require full disability, while others pay benefits for only partial disability. Careful understanding of the specific benefits, including the *definition of disability in the policy being purchased,* is a must. A wife should be just as much aware of the disability insurance on a husband as he is, because if disability happens, she and the children will be just as much affected as the husband, and it is usually the wife who will have to actually make the claim *for* her disabled husband.

HOW SHOULD THE RISK OF LAWSUITS BE MANAGED? The answer is that they can be covered in your "property and casualty" insurance. That means in your homeowner's, your automobile, and your business insurance policies. Or, this risk can be covered in a type of policy called an "umbrella" policy, a kind of master policy with many types of coverage included in it. These kinds of policies are no more important to have than life insurance, but a surprising number of Americans routinely carry this kind of protection through insurance, while neglecting to have life insurance or disability insurance. This may be because some states refuse to license cars or drivers without proof of insurance, and most people with homes are afraid of losing their investment in their homes to fire damage, so they carry homeowner's and auto insurance with no hesitation, but these same people frequently have no life insurance on the parents in a family.

My personal opinion is that while it is good that people have to have liability insurance in their auto and homeowner's insurance policies, we would do folks a favor if we could also require that "if you are going to get married, you will have to have proof of life-insurance coverage." This is an absurd idea, of course, and would never be passed as a law, but I make my point that it is just as important, perhaps more so, to own life insurance as homeowner's and auto insurance. It is not mandated by law, however, so many people simply do not buy it. It appears that driving their cars is more important to some people than protecting their families by owning adequate life insurance on the breadwinner.

Renters, by the way, can purchase "renter's insurance" that can include liability coverage to protect you in the event that someone is injured on your property. It also insures you from losses of your personal property, furniture, and so forth, in the event of fire, theft, and other hazards.

SOLUTION #2: START AND MAINTAIN A SAVINGS PLAN

Everyone who takes a job should start and maintain a payroll-savings plan with the first paycheck he/she receives, from day one. It has proven true time and time again that if it isn't included in your paycheck, you won't miss it, and you will manage fine without it, especially in a country as affluent as America.

Let me give you an example with which I am very familiar—my own situation twenty-five years ago. I was a young, single mom with two preschool children. I had a job in a bank (my first), and my take-home pay was $340 per month (really!).

I had been awarded the family home in a divorce, but I also had to make the payments on it. I was supposed to receive child support of $150 per month but did not get it regularly after the first year. I did not know how to enforce the payment of child support and just gave up. Like many divorced moms today, I had to manage without it.

My father had always taught me to save, so when I took my very first job, I signed up for the payroll-savings plan they offered, in which I saved a grand total of five dollars per month. Not a monumental amount, to be sure, but it was a start, and God honored it. My five dollars was taken out of my paycheck and went into a savings account for me; it came out of my paycheck before I even got the paycheck, and I never saw the five dollars, nor missed it.

My expenses were so simple: a house payment of $110 per month, $40 per month for taxes and homeowner's insurance, child care of $20 per week ($80 per month . . . just like today, child care is almost as much as a mortgage payment), and utilities of about $55 per month (including heat and phone). That left me with $65 per month for groceries and miscellaneous expenses. Pretty slim. . . .

I had no car, so I had no car expenses. I rode the bus to work. I walked my children to the baby-sitter one block away. I walked to the bus stop about a mile away. I got up early every day, and I got to work on time.

I had no credit cards (who would have given me credit?) and no charge accounts at department stores. It was too much work to take the bus to the mall, so I never shopped there. I could not afford to, anyway. We ate a lot of inexpensive cuts of meat, and I cooked everything from scratch. Life was not complicated; I could not afford any complications.

After a couple of years of this kind of simple living, my father gave me three hundred dollars and insisted that I buy a car with it. I bought a little car that I decided to use only for emergencies, such as trips to the doctor, because I really could not afford to keep gas in the car. I continued to walk or use the bus for most of my transportation. Now, however, my kids could go on an occasional camping trip, which we did once in a while for fun.

Eventually, I got raises and earned more money. I remarried a few years later. My situation gradually improved, but I remember those lean years well. My children never realized that we were so poor; they never suffered from it at all. They joke today about eating a lot of hot dogs and peanut butter as small kids, but to this day they don't know why that is significant. They had enough toys, mostly from Grandma and Grandpa; they had clothing, mostly from thrift stores, and they ate every day. They played and went to school like other kids, and they went to the doctor a couple of times, once for a cut that needed stitches and other times for routine shots at the county health department (it was much cheaper there). I had medical insurance, which my employer paid for, but it did not pay for the first $250 of expenses, so I had to pay for these visits to the doctor myself. I did this with the five dollars per month that I had saved in my little payroll-savings plan account.

God honored my need to support and care for my children because I was trying very hard to be responsible. I managed what little I had very carefully, and I saved every month. The principle of saving *saved me* . . . more than once. God stepped in repeatedly *after* I proved that I was doing all that I could do.

SOLUTION #3: PAY OFF YOUR MORTGAGE EARLY

You can reverse a decline in your net worth by setting up a plan to pay off your mortgage ahead of time. This works if you can pay off one or more bills, then use the extra money you now have to pay against the principal of your mortgage, thereby paying it off early.

What is the "principal" of your mortgage? I am often asked that question. The answer is that when you get a mortgage to buy a home, you borrow a certain amount, say, seventy-five thousand dollars at a certain interest rate. This seventy-five thousand dollars is the "principal" of your mortgage, the amount initially borrowed. It is not, however, the amount you will repay over time. That amount will be much greater, as much as three times the principal, depending on the interest rate of your mortgage. The higher the interest rate, the greater the total you will pay over the years. The principal goes down as you pay off the mortgage monthly. The monthly mortgage amount is your house payment. You usually have twenty-five to thirty years to repay this.

Your house payment consists of principal *plus* interest. This is because your loan is charged interest, which is how the bank makes money from lending to you so that you can buy the home. You pay interest on the unpaid balance of your loan. There are several ways to actually calculate this interest. This calculation is called the "amortization schedule."

Most of the interest is charged in the first fifteen years of a thirty-year loan. Therefore, most of your house payments in the first fifteen years will be interest, not the original seventy-five thousand dollars of principal that you borrowed. This increases the true cost of that home by two or three times what you paid to buy the home.

By paying off the principal early, you can gain several advantages. First, you pay off the home early, often cutting the number of years in half. Second, you do not pay nearly as much interest as you would have if you paid off the home in thirty years instead of the shorter period.

If you plan to stay in your home for a long time, possibly until retirement, this is a good plan, because you can pay off your home and owe nothing on it at retirement, thereby having that much extra on which to live in retirement, once you are no longer making house payments.

I know of no banks or mortgage lenders that will not allow you to pay extra amounts against the principal. They cannot prohibit this practice. You simply make your regular monthly payment and then write a second check for the extra that you wish to pay, attach a note that the extra amount is to "be applied to principal only." This should also be noted on the face of the check. By the amount of this extra payment, the bank will then reduce your principal owed.

SOLUTION #4: REFINANCE YOUR HOME

This is not for everyone, but it does solve problems in some cases. Be very careful about trying this, as I have seen some people use this strategy and end up in worse financial condition than they started in. Study this concept carefully first to determine if it is okay for you to do, and do it only if you are absolutely certain that you won't abuse this strategy.

To *refinance* merely means to get a new mortgage, preferably at better terms and a lower interest rate, which will usually reduce your house payment. The old mortgage will be paid off by the new one, and you will start over again in your house payments, but they will be less than before.

This is how this strategy works: Let's say that your mortgage is for seventy-five thousand dollars and the interest rate is 12 percent. You bought your home eight years ago and have twenty-two years left to pay on the loan. You put five thousand dollars down payment on it and have payments of $720 per month (principal and interest), plus you pay $150 per month for taxes and insurance.

Over the last eight years, your seventy-five thousand dollar home has doubled in value. Because of this, the bank is very willing to refinance your loan. You currently owe $66,500 on your loan. You are interested in refinancing this $66,500 that you now owe on the home, but no more than this amount. You find out that if you can refinance the entire loan at 9 percent, your mortgage payments would drop to $535 per month, which you could use to pay off bills, pay down your mortgage early by paying extra on the principal, or save in a savings account.

You find out that the bank will charge you a 1.5% "loan fee" which is due up-front, to be able to get this refinance loan. You do not have this 1.5% fee, which amounts to $998, so the bank offers to add that $998 to the refinance loan, which most banks are happy to do.

Now you are not out-of-pocket any cash, but your loan will be for $67,498 that you now owe instead of $66,500. This is okay in this case, because your payments will still be much lower. The payments on $67,498 at 9 percent will be about $543 per month, still a savings of $177 per month over the current monthly payment.

Now you take the $177 per month saved and put it to good use. Let's say that you have $2,500 in debts that you want to pay off, and you have no savings, which worries you. You can attack both problems at once, or one at a time. If you decide to attack both at once, let's assume that you decide to pay off the $2,500 of debt with one hundred dollars per month over what you are already paying on this debt. Assuming that you *cut up the credit cards* that made this debt possible, and assuming that you are already paying twenty-five dollars per month on the bill, you now will be able to pay one hundred twenty-five dollars per month and have the entire debt paid off completely in about one year and nine months, even at an 18 percent interest rate (common on credit cards). The $77 that you have left each month from the $177 being saved from the lower house payment can be put into a savings account. At 5.5% interest, this savings account will grow to over two thousand dollars in only two years. *This is a very good start to an adequate emergency fund! You are now well on your way to good money management!*

God will honor this effort on your part. You will gradually gain confidence and satisfaction from your stewardship, and God will bless you with a new sense of peace about financial matters. He may even bless you financially.

Once you have paid off the $2,500 debt entirely, you can begin to apply one hundred dollars per month to the new principal on your new mortgage. This will knock many years off from your new mortgage, as much as ten or fifteen years, meaning that the new thirty-year mortgage will now be paid off in fifteen or twenty years, still less than the twenty-two years that you had left on the original mortgage.

This is a pretty good plan, IF all of the numbers are carefully calculated in advance, and IF it all "pencils out" on paper before you sign on the dotted line.

SOLUTION #5: SELL ALL AND START OVER

If you want to, and agree that it really is the best solution, you can sell all of your assets, pay off all of your debts, pay any taxes you will owe on any gains you have made (such as gains on the sale of your home), and just start over.

Remember, however, that if your net worth is *negative*, you will still owe money to someone even after selling all of your assets. You will still have to pay off what you owe.

Sometimes this is not a good solution because sometimes it means that your living expenses are actually going to increase instead of decrease. Be very careful about resorting to selling everything to get out of debt.

EXAMPLE: selling your home to get out of debt. Unless your home has appreciated enough in value to pay off all of your debts, you will find that selling it does not solve your problem. This is because your house payment may be less than the rent you will have to pay after you sell and move to a rental place. Rents are high in some parts of the country. If this is true where you live, think this idea through before you leap to conclusions that selling is a good idea for you. If you live in a small town, or have some way of getting really cheap rent, this might be a solution to your problem, but not otherwise.

Also, don't forget that when you sell a home for more than you paid for it, you make a profit on it and will owe taxes to the IRS on that profit (unless you buy another house for at least as much as you sold the old house). Not all of the proceeds from the sale of your house will be yours to keep; the IRS will get some of your profits. You have now acquired a *new debt*, called "taxes due," which you will have to pay on your next income tax return. Currently, the (1995) tax rate that you would pay on this gain is 28 percent. If your gain is a profit of twenty thousand dollars, you will owe $5,600 in taxes. If you have twenty thousand dollars in debts that you wanted to pay off with the twenty thousand dollars profit, be forewarned that you will only be able to use $14,400 to pay toward your debts, because Uncle Sam will get the other $5,600.

5
USING A BUDGET

I like to refer to a budget as a "spending plan" instead of the dreaded term, *budget*. It is like calling a diet an "eating plan," and it makes it easier to swallow (no pun intended).

A *spending plan* is, in fact, a more accurate term to use. You are not planning a way to restrict your use of money but instead are planning how to spend it wisely and have a little left over. A spending plan fits with the overall strategy of being in control of your life, and your money, too. So start thinking in those terms and agree to take this seriously.

A workable budget, or spending plan, is key to being in control of your finances instead of letting them control you. Large corporations require budgets, *for good reasons, in order to stay in business, and so should your household*.

By building a workable budget, you will discover that as a Christian, you have several categories of expense that a non-Christian does not have. You also, however, have the promise of blessings that the non-Christian will not enjoy. Some of these blessings are material, and some are spiritual. Either is reward enough for me.

One of the expenses that non-Christians do not have is the tithe. Christians need to tithe, as much for their own sake as for any other reason. The tithe should be built into their budget from the beginning, regardless of how much financial trouble you are in. Curb your expenses somewhere else . . . or *everywhere* else if necessary, but don't cut back on your tithe just because you have some financial problems. This does not mean that you cannot tithe a smaller amount when your income declines to a smaller amount. It simply means that the tithe should not be the first category of expense to forego when you run into a financial squeeze. The principal is what is important here, not so much the dollar amount.

I often hear from Christians in financial trouble that they "would like to tithe but just can't afford to." I certainly understand what they are saying, as I can do the math as well as the next person, and sometimes there really isn't enough money to go around. However, I believe that God will and does honor our willingness to tithe under these kinds of circumstances, far beyond our ability to understand how we could possibly tithe and still pay our bills.

The tithe is an issue of trust, not money. It is not a one-way issue. I have heard many times that "you must trust God with and for your finances." True, true, true! But you must *also* prove that *you*, likewise, can be trusted by God. It is a two-way street. *You* must trust, and *you* must be trustworthy.

By paying the tithe, you are stating loudly and clearly to God that you trust Him so much that you are willing to be a trustworthy and dependable giver despite your circumstances. This is when the blessings will come, when your giving is during difficult financial situations, showing that you trust even when you "cannot afford to."

God performs spectacular miracles when you trust Him that much and show Him how truly trustworthy you are, as well. Some of those miracles will be inside of *yourself*, not in your pocketbook or checking account. Sometimes, *God cares more about you, in your heart, than about your money.* If you tithe and stay in financial trouble, you must understand that in a way we cannot understand, God is still working on your situation, but it may be that He is working directly on *you*, not your finances, as the ultimate solution to your problems.

So you are ready to set up your budget-spending plan now. By agreeing to pay the tithe and the income taxes that you owe, you have now "spent" about 25 percent of your gross income, maybe more.

For example, if your salary is three thousand dollars per month, and your taxes of $450 per month are taken directly out of your paycheck, this leaves you with $2,550. Your tithe is ten percent of $2,550 or $255 per month. Some people prefer to tithe on their gross; in that case, the tithe would be ten percent of the three thousand dollars or three hundred dollars per month.

Using the 10 percent tithe on gross of three thousand dollars, your budget would follow like this:

You start with three thousand dollars per month, then subtract three hundred dollars for tithe and $450 for taxes. That leaves you with $2,250, or 75 percent of your original amount, on which to live each month. This is the amount that you will want to work with in your budget-spending plan. This is only an example, of course. You will have to figure out exactly your own amounts for yourself, using whatever percentages apply to your situation in particular. I have used the 25 percent as an example, but it is a low example percentage. It is the correct amount for someone in the lowest income tax bracket of only 15 percent. If you are in the 28 percent tax bracket, the correct percentage will be 38 percent that you will "spend" on taxes and tithe combined, before setting up your budget. For someone in the 31 percent tax bracket, the amount spent on taxes and tithe will be 41 percent . . . and so on. Below are the current (1995) income levels at each tax bracket. Find yours to determine what your tax bracket is:

Married Couples & Surviving Spouses Singles

up to $39,000 = 15% bracket	up to $23,350 = 15% bracket
$39,000 to $94,250 = 28% bracket	$23,350 to $56,550 = 28% bracket
$94,250 to $143,600 = 31% bracket	$56,550 to $117,950 = 31% bracket
$143,600 to $256,500 = 36% bracket	$117,950 to $256,500 = 36% bracket
over $256,500 = 39.6% bracket	over $256,500 = 39.6% bracket

Heads of household rates are better than single but not as good as married, and married filing separate rates are worse even than single taxpayer rates. These change frequently.

HOW MUCH SHOULD CERTAIN EXPENSES BE? I am often asked this question: "How much should we be paying for food?" or "How much should our house payment be?" The answers are going to vary from family to family, but there are some averages that you can consider in putting your own budget together. If you have a *good* reason not to fit the average in a particular category, do not attempt to conform in that expense category.

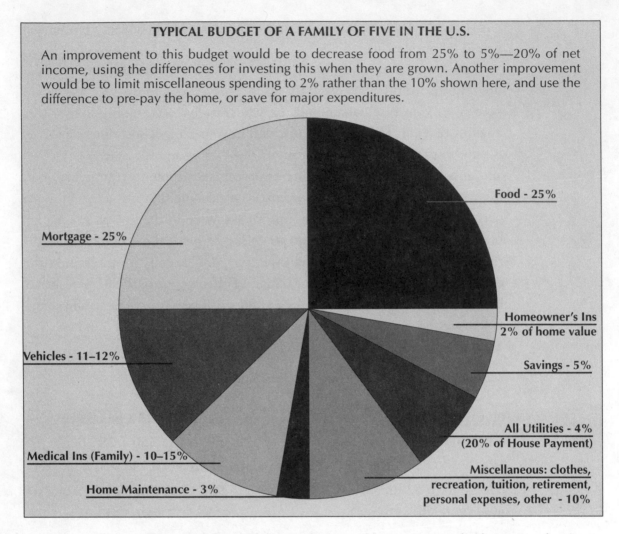

TYPICAL BUDGET OF A FAMILY OF FIVE IN THE U.S.

An improvement to this budget would be to decrease food from 25% to 5%—20% of net income, using the differences for investing this when they are grown. Another improvement would be to limit miscellaneous spending to 2% rather than the 10% shown here, and use the difference to pre-pay the home, or save for major expenditures.

Food - 25%

Mortgage - 25%

Homeowner's Ins
2% of home value

Savings - 5%

Vehicles - 11–12%

All Utilities - 4%
(20% of House Payment)

Medical Ins (Family) - 10–15%

Miscellaneous: clothes,
recreation, tuition, retirement,
personal expenses, other - 10%

Home Maintenance - 3%

For example, if you have chronic and ongoing medical expense that is not entirely covered by health insurance, you may find yourself spending more in that category than the average person. When this happens, it is not an excuse to overspend in a budget, however. It simply means that you will have to spend less in some other category because of being forced to overspend in the medical expense category. You may think that this is "unfair," but life is that way sometimes. If it isn't fair, so be it, but *you still have to stay within your budget*. I had a client one time with that kind of problem, and she complained bitterly about the "unfairness" of her own situation—but she never got control of her problem, and so it never went away. Complaining about your problem's

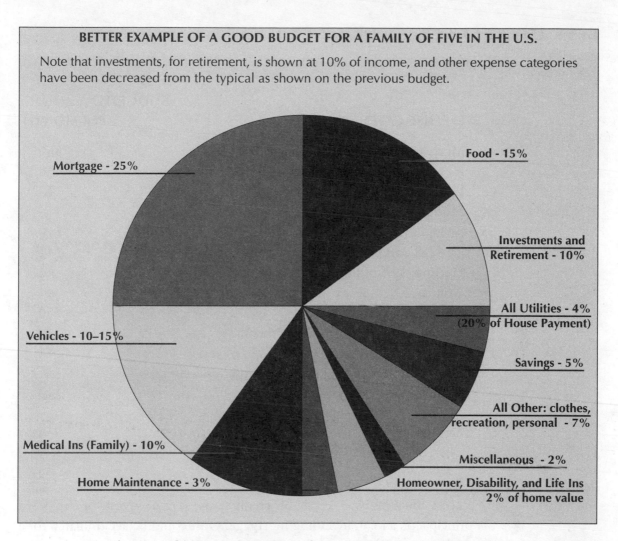

BETTER EXAMPLE OF A GOOD BUDGET FOR A FAMILY OF FIVE IN THE U.S.

Note that investments, for retirement, is shown at 10% of income, and other expense categories have been decreased from the typical as shown on the previous budget.

- Mortgage - 25%
- Food - 15%
- Investments and Retirement - 10%
- All Utilities - 4% (20% of House Payment)
- Savings - 5%
- Vehicles - 10–15%
- All Other: clothes, recreation, personal - 7%
- Miscellaneous - 2%
- Medical Ins (Family) - 10%
- Homeowner, Disability, and Life Ins 2% of home value
- Home Maintenance - 3%

being unfair is simply a waste of time, so just do something about it and let go of the complaints.

Now you can look over this list below of average expenses in the typical American budget. This is only a starting point, not an ending. Begin here and work with your figures *until they make sense.* Your commitment to this part of the process of financial planning and your sacrificial tithe in spite of your circumstances will demonstrate clearly that *you* are *trustworthy.* God will work miraculous wonders on your behalf, not because you deserve help (you do not) but because *He is full of mercy.*

LIST OF AVERAGE BUDGET EXPENSES

Example: assume gross monthly income of $3000, net of $2,200, family of five.

EXPENSE CATEGORY	BUDGETED AMOUNT PER MONTH
1. Mortgage, 25% of net income	$ 550
2. Home maintenance, 3% of net income	66
3. Homeowner insurance, .2% of home value of $85,000	15
4. Mortgage insurance*	-0-
5. Savings, 5% of net income	110
6. Cars (all costs), 11% of net income	242
7. Heating, 12% of house payment	66
8. Utilities, 8% of house payment	44
9. Food, 25% of net income	550
10. Medical insurance, 10% of net income	220
11. Recreation, 2% of net income	44
12. Miscellaneous, gasoline, stamps, subscriptions, clothing, extras, 5% of net income	110
TOTAL	$ 2,017
*******EXCESS *******	$183

Excess could be used to pay off credit cards, save or invest, or pay down the principal on a loan, including mortgage. Or it could be accumulated for a planned purchase that you will need, to avoid using credit to make that purchase.

---

*Don't buy, use life insurance instead.

6 TIPS ON REDUCING EXPENSES

Part of making a budget work, perhaps the biggest part, is reducing your household expenses where possible. It usually is much harder to increase income than to reduce expenses, so this area, reducing expenses, is the first place to start in making up a realistic spending plan.

Too often, people with financial problems think that they can do nothing to spend less. They tell me that they are "trapped" with the expenses that they now have and feel that they cannot spend less. *This is simply not true.*

There are several creative ways to reduce your household expenses. The following list of tips is *not* a total list of ways to reduce your expenses; you may think of something not listed here. If so, add your own ideas to this list. In fact, mail them to me, and I will add them to the list when this book is updated! *Be creative!*

Reducing your spending in these ways, and other ways that you will undoubtedly think of, is part of the creative process of gaining control of your finances. There are so many things that *you can do* that you will be amazed, once you make the firm commitment to do so. One final note before I list the cost-cutting tips listed below—remember that spending less when you have been used to spending more does not mean that your standard of living will go down, or that you, or your family, must do without. What it *does* mean is that you will reevaluate your lifestyle and respond to your problems creatively. Be willing to make some sacrifices now in order to enjoy a better future. Be willing to give up some of the little comforts that you never questioned until now.

Be ready, as a result, to live better by living without financial bondage. This is a true measure of the value of your lifestyle, and it is definitely the best kind of lifestyle to enjoy, one free of financial bondage, despite the sacrifices that it will entail.

Here is a list that will get you thinking of how you can reduce your expenses:

1. Stay out of malls, shopping centers, and stores! Be "too busy to shop"!
2. When you must shop, shop at thrift stores and garage sales. This can be fun, and it will also save you a lot of money.
3. Shop only for necessities. You really do not need the extras right now. Your goal in shopping, or not shopping, is to learn *discipline*. Skip the extras until later on.
4. When you *must* shop, determine in advance how much you can spend. Take only that amount of money and no more, in cash.
5. When you cannot find what you want to purchase, do not purchase a "substitute item" just to satisfy your need to buy. Commit only to buying an item when you need that exact item at the price you can afford. If you cannot find it for that price, you don't need it.
6. Can, freeze, and dry your own food if you have a garden. Reuse canning jars and freezer bags (used also for dried foods). You can buy canning jars at garage sales for a fraction of the price of new ones in the store.
7. Plant a garden for fruits and vegetables and use it for food supplies. The extra work is worth it and the superior quality of these home-grown foods will amaze you; you will save a lot of money and be too busy gardening to shop.
8. Plant an herb garden and dry your herbs and spices. These items are *very* expensive in the store. A small herb garden, if tended, can yield enough herbs and spices, when dried and stored, to supply your family for one to two years of seasonings. Growing your own will relieve your budget of these very costly grocery expenses.
9. Shop for groceries only on a set schedule. Do not make "quick trips" to the store for items you forgot. Do without those items until your

regularly scheduled grocery-shopping trip comes around. Never shop for groceries when you are hungry!

10. Freeze leftover foods for soups and stews. Use these leftovers religiously during each week, with a "leftover meal" planned in advance. Food that cannot be used in this way can often be used as compost for next year's garden.

11. Prepare your own baby foods from adult meals prepared. Mash by hand if you do not have a blender, and store several days' worth in the refrigerator for baby.

12. Cook with powdered milk and meat substitutes to save money on fresh milk and meats. Check out some vegetarian and "healthy heart" cookbooks from your local library to get wonderful new recipes for cooking without expensive meats.

13. Prepare a weekly menu of meals and a weekly shopping list from the meals planned. Take both with you when you shop, buying only what is on your list.

14. In grocery stores, shop primarily on the "outside rim" of the store. Stay out of the aisles as much as possible. The best foods are on the "rim"; the prepared, expensive, and less healthful foods are in the aisles.

15. Use a Crock-Pot for slow cooking the least expensive cuts of meats and for beans, rice, stews, one-dish meals, and for making soup stocks. Cook bones in the slow-cooking process to get stocks for use in soups and as a base for other meals.

16. Investigate and become familiar with the services of your local library, especially the reference desk and the "how-to" section. These resources will tell you how to maintain your home, repair things, buy things on sale, keep your car(s) running longer, and make things like furniture, clothes, tools, garden equipment (like a compost bin), and so forth.

17. Don't be afraid to try to make something that you need. And don't believe that you have to purchase new wood or tools to build things. You can get excellent-quality material by shopping for these things secondhand. I know of one family who got the wood for their new house from a condemned house being torn down, and I know

another family who salvaged an old giant pickle barrel from a pickle factory and made it into a hot tub on the deck that they built. They had a little trouble with the pickle smell for about a year but finally figured out how to get rid of that and have a great hot tub for zero dollars! And we had a great time laughing over the fact that they were pickled for over a year! I know another family that bought all of their garden tools at a barn sale and got farmer-quality rakes, hoes, etcetera, at less than a dollar per tool. I know of a family who offered to haul away the wooden doors of a university that was building a new wing after tearing down the old wing; they used those beautiful wooden doors in the home they were building on a tight budget, and they got the doors for nothing.

18. If you plan to purchase real estate, get the list of repossessed homes and properties from your local bank or realtor. They will probably be happy to give it to you. If not, go to another bank or realtor, as some make a specific market in repossessed real estate. These homes are steeply discounted and can be purchased for far less than value. Sometimes they can be purchased for just the back taxes due. Most will need work, however, so be prepared to do some fix-up. Another place to find discounted real estate is through estate sales, the kind that are the result of a death and a family's needing to sell a property fast to pay taxes due at death.

19. Inquire at your local police department about sheriff's sales and auctions also. Sometimes, local law enforcement agencies have sales at very low prices on a variety of items, often the "big-ticket" items. Often, however, you will have to be prepared to pay cash.

20. Use cloth diapers. Paper diapers are *very* expensive and create tremendous waste.

21. Take sack lunches to work, or leftovers from your home-cooked meals if you have access to a microwave where you work.

22. Skip the planned vacation this year. Go camping instead. Borrow any needed equipment and *return same in perfect condition*.

23. Check videos out of the local library instead of video stores.

24. Turn off the TV and disconnect the cable. Use the time not spent watching TV to make gifts instead of buying presents, and for cook-

ing from scratch. Let your kids start to learn to cook, too, using the time they used to spend watching TV for cooking lessons.

25. Put on a sweater and turn down the heat in your home.

26. Seal up the heat leaks in your home. Wrap your water heater. Turn your water heater down to a safe, less-costly temperature.

27. Co-op your baby-sitting with another family that also wants to work on their budget and has kids that can play with your kids. The kids will love it, and you will save money.

28. Discontinue buying all processed foods.

29. Stay out of fast-food restaurants.

30. Buy generic brands, including prescriptions, when available.

31. Ask for cash discounts on purchases that advertise that they will give you credit. Go for 15 percent less.

32. Be your own contractor on building projects, even if you hire someone, and ask for the contractor's prices on construction items you buy.

33. Keep warranty records and request free repairs on items still under warranty when they break down. It amazes me how many people pay for repairs on appliances and electronic equipment that are still under warranty because the warranty was thrown out.

34. Avoid buying the "luxury model."

35. Avoid the dealer-service contracts that are pushed on appliances or electronic gadgets. They are sometimes worth having on a car or a computer, however.

36. Turn down the "opportunity" to buy credit insurance on items that you buy through a loan, such as a car loan or a mortgage. If you need insurance to cover your debts, buy only life insurance to pay in case of death. If you need it to make the payments if you lost your job, you can't afford the item you are buying.

37. Sell your old car yourself instead of trading it in as a down payment on a new car. You will get more for it if you do this.

38. Go to the library and find out the manufacturer's wholesale price of a car, or other big-ticket item, before you shop for this kind of thing. Offer the car dealer a set amount over the manufacturer's wholesale price. Don't buy from a car dealer who will not agree to sell to you

on this basis. Get up and leave his office and buy your car somewhere else.

39. Buy year-end demo cars, or salesmen's models, with very low mileage and new-car warranties still in effect, in November and December.

40. Offer to buy a car at dealer wholesale from a dealer who is in a sales contest. Tell the dealer ahead of time what kind of car you are looking for and ask him to call you if he needs to sell that kind of car, wholesale, just to win a contest. Some dealers will call you back, and you will get the car you want for thousands of dollars less than regular price just because the dealer wanted to win a sales contest by selling one more car—to you!

41. Keep your old car repaired and do routine maintenance when due. Poorly maintained cars break down more often and are worth less when you want to sell them.

42. Cancel magazine subscriptions and newspapers. Listen to the news on the radio instead, while driving or working around your home.

43. Limit unnecessary visits to the doctor or dentist. Doctors tell me often that most of the patients that they see will get better by themselves without the attention of a physician. Be wise here and use your discernment skills, however. Go when it is truly necessary, such as with signs of heart attack (most people wait too long with chest pain), or serious illness or accidents. Don't run to the doctor for the flu, a cold, a small cut or scrape, or the little things that generally resolve themselves in a few days.

44. Don't ask your doctor to prescribe medicines that he or she is reluctant to prescribe, such as antibiotics that are only marginally effective, or pain medication for a temporary problem, or other drugs that you may not really need.

45. Keep a daily spending diary. This will tell you a real story, sometimes a "horror story," in a few months!

46. Establish a set limit on buying for unplanned purchases, per month. **DON'T CHEAT!**

47. Cut up all your credit cards and charge-account cards. Write a letter to all your creditors, telling them you are going to work on paying down your cards and charge accounts and that you intend to discon-

tinue using your cards for a while so that you can accomplish this goal. Ask their cooperation in keeping your account available so that you can use it again after you pay them off entirely. Then *pay the entire bill monthly* when you start using cards and charge accounts again.

48. Do not take your kids to the grocery store when you shop, or to the mall or department stores. Leave them with a co-op baby-sitter when you shop. Reward them by *playing* with them, at home, in the park, wherever, when you get home if they were good while you were gone.

49. Make up games to play with your kids instead of buying toys. Let them make up some of the games and play them even when the games are really dumb.

50. Read to your kids and have them read to you instead of watching TV nightly. Get them their own library card and make regular weekly trips to the library. Reward them for reading and create incentives for them to read.

51. Stop driving your kids to school. If necessary, such as with private school, start a car pool of parents. *Don't give your teenager a car*, especially a teenage boy, unless he or she earns his or her own money with which to buy the car and can pay for his or her own gas, insurance, and car tabs yearly.

52. Make a "savings goal." For example, decide to spend 5 percent less on groceries; i.e., if your normal grocery budget is four hundred dollars, reduce it by 5 percent or 10 percent. Do the same in other categories. You will be amazed at how easy it is to spend less in each category once you have a written goal and decide to stick with it.

53. Exchange names at Christmas for gifts, buying only one gift for one person instead of many gifts for multiple persons. Too many Americans spend far too much at Christmastime. Put the real meaning back into Christmas and opt out of the buying frenzy.

54. Agree among your family members to a limit on what is spent for gifts for all occasions, then stick with that limit.

55. Barter as often as possible for goods and services when you can arrange them. For example, if you have gardening skills, offer to plant

a garden for a mechanic in return for having him tune your car. Figure out what skills you have and go looking for barter partners so you can get goods and services without spending cash.

THE RESULTS of using these kinds of cost-saving strategies will begin to pay handsome dividends in about six months. In addition, you will find yourself less tempted to spend. You will *not* shop habitually, a serious financial disease among many, many people in this country!

If your reduced spending produces an overall savings of 5 percent of your total household expenses, use that savings to begin to pay off debts, or to start a savings plan. For example, if you had previously been spending two thousand dollars per month to run your household, a 5 percent annual savings would amount to $1,200 in only one year! If you had saved this money at only 6 percent interest, in ten years you would have accumulated $16,767 just from this budget-trimming process alone. This is no small amount! *Budget cuts do work!*

7 WHAT HAPPENS IF THE BREADWINNER DIES?

*T*hink about it, as awful as it is: What will happen to you, to your children, your home, your family if your husband dies suddenly? Don't kid yourself by saying that "he is too young" or "it won't happen to us." It does happen, every day.

I know of countless women who are widowed in their twenties, or thirties, or forties, while still at home having babies and raising children. I can tell numerous stories of women whose husbands died unexpectedly, from a car accident, a heart attack, a hunting accident, a strange illness, while skin-diving, boating, hiking, taking a shower. None of these women had even a clue that one day they would be married and the next day widowed. Most were totally unprepared, totally ignorant of what would happen to them and their children if their husband died. Their stories won't cheer you up, but they are true, and they happen every day, every week, every month, all across this country.

In my seminars and frequent media talk shows, I tell men and women alike, jokingly (to take the somber edge off of the topic of death), that the biggest lie that men tell their wives is "*Don't worry, honey, it's all taken care of.*" Most men chuckle when I say that, but it is not really funny. The truth is, it is NOT *all taken care of.*

Without wills, without adequate life insurance, without a budget, without a retirement plan and an estate plan, premature death of the family breadwinner can result in more than loss of the person; it can also be the reason for the family to lose everything else besides the husband and father.

WHAT PAPERWORK ACTUALLY HAPPENS AT DEATH?

First, you will need to get copies of the death certificate; usually ten to twelve certified copies are enough. Every place that you have ownership, jointly or not, with your husband, on any asset, will require proof of his death in order to change the title from your joint names to your name only. This is not true on bank accounts, of course, because you simply go in and close any bank accounts held in joint name and reopen in your own name alone. But on real estate, vehicles, boats, business assets, and so forth that you owned jointly, you will have to have proof of his death before you can remove his name from the title. Why is this important?

Because you may want, or be forced, to sell that asset. Even if you do not plan to sell now, or in the near future, you will probably want to sell it later, and to do so you will have to have it in your name. The reason is that you cannot sell something you don't own, and your title is your proof of ownership. If you wait until your own death to pass it to your heirs but have never changed the title, they will have to go through an expensive, long legal process with attorney fees and title fees, just to search, change title, and receive the asset you meant to pass along to them at your death. It is a difficult process that your heirs will not enjoy having to do, and it will only happen because you left them some asset that was incorrectly titled, with questionable ownership.

At death, you will need to notify your husband's employer, his pension plan(s), his previous employers, in case that there is a pension through former employers as well as the current one, Social Security, the military (if he had a service record), all banks, all real-estate title companies involved in your real estate, all investment companies and all insurance companies with which he had policies. There may be additional places that you will want to notify and also send certified death certificates to.

WHY? Because you will need to find out if you are the beneficiary of any proceeds from life insurance, pension lump sums, pension income, or other death benefits from an employer or a union, and you will need to become sole owner of all of the assets that your husband previously signed on, such as bank accounts, investments, houses, cars, and so forth. You may need income, and this is the only way for you to find out if you will be eligible for any income from these sources.

 Once you determine what you have in assets from all of these sources, you and a financial planner will have to calculate if these assets can produce income, and if so, how much for what period of time. This is the starting point at which cold reality sets in for many new widows. I have had to tell a number of them that they will not get any income, period, because there were not enough assets, just a house and some debts. The next question is always "What am I going to do now?" The answer is that the new widow will have to get a job, or sell the family home, or remarry fast.

WHAT CHOICES DO YOU HAVE IF THE BREADWINNER DIES?

Below is a list of what you can do to survive financially if your spouse dies:

1. Live off the proceeds from life insurance
2. Live off Social Security income if you can get it
3. Live off income from investments if you have them
4. Live off pension benefits if you can get them
5. Get a job
6. Sell your home and live off the income from it
7. Remarry
8. Move in with family or friends
9. Go on welfare

Okay, now let's look at SOME of these options separately:

GETTING A JOB: While this is the reality for most women who, with their husbands, did no financial planning, the real question is whether or not you are truly employable. Ask yourself the following questions:

- Can I work? At what jobs?
- How much can I earn?
- How much will I need to live?
- What additional expenses will I have if I go to work?

Don't let your husband tell you that you can "always go to work" if you have to, unless you know for certain that this is true and that you could earn enough to actually live on what you could earn. For some reason, many men and women use this logic as an excuse for not buying life insurance or facing this important issue. It does not hold water as a reason for failing to do either.

How much life insurance should you have? Any breadwinner should carry enough life insurance to cover the cost of maintaining the family home, plus education expenses, for his or her family. This amounts to about eight to twelve times your annual expenses.

EXAMPLE OF HOW MUCH LIFE INSURANCE IS NEEDED

Example: Monthly expenses are $2000 x 12 = 24,000 (annual amount) x 12 = 288,000 of life insurance needed for 12 times expenses. I will use $200,000 as my example. However, if you have already saved fifty thousand dollars and it is not needed for something specific, you will only need one hundred fifty thousand dollars in life insurance, of the two hundred thousand dollars needed. DON'T count on your home as an asset in this calculation; it is not usually the kind of asset that you can just sell and live off the income, as you will still need a place to live.

If you have no children, you can probably use the figure of eight times your annual expenses instead of multiplying your annual expenses times ten or twelve. But if you have a large family, the expenses of children indicate that you will need to use the figure of twelve times your annual expenses instead of ten, and so on.

Life insurance provided by your employer is not enough and should NOT be the only life insurance that you have. You could lose that job or leave for another job. You might take a job that offers no life insurance, or you might become uninsurable due to medical conditions. For all of these reasons, get your own policy now and keep it up.

SHOULD YOU BUY TERM INSURANCE OR PERMANENT INSURANCE?

I am always asked this question. There is considerable disagreement among financial professionals as to which is the "right" kind of insurance to own. I do not think that the answer is a simple one, as your situation will be unique, making the selection of the type of insurance plan unique also. Let me explain:

TERM INSURANCE: is temporary and inexpensive, at least until age forty-five to fifty. It only provides the death benefit that the policy states and only in the event of death. The cost of the insurance premium is based solely on the risk of death, called "mortality risk." Term insurance is usually purchased when protection is the only goal.

Because it is less expensive than other types of insurance policies, term insurance is generally the type purchased by employers for the group policies provided to employees, and is often the best kind of insurance for young families with a big need but little income.

Term insurance goes up in price each year because it is based only on age and health. The older you are, or the poorer your health, the more expensive the insurance will be.

Once you buy term insurance, you have to continue to pay the premiums each month and each year to have continuous protection. You cannot "pay up" a term policy, which is where it gets the name "temporary insurance." If you stop paying premiums, your coverage stops. If you continue to pay premiums, your coverage continues, regardless of your health, which may have gone bad.

You cannot increase the amount of the death benefit in a term policy without buying another policy. Term insurance is relatively inexpensive for the very young person but becomes rather more expensive for the older person. At about age forty-five, term insurance can become as expensive as permanent insurance, which makes this age a good time to switch from term to permanent insurance. A problem, however, that often occurs is that by the time it is financially advantageous to switch, you are no longer in good enough health to qualify for the new policy. This is why some people prefer to buy the more expensive permanent insurance at a young age.

I recommend, with either type of policy, term or permanent, that you think far into the future and consider inflation by buying more than you need today. Instead, buy what you think you will need in twenty years, to be sure to have enough protection after twenty years of inflation. This means that if fifty thousand dollars would be enough today, you really should buy two hundred fifty thousand dollars if you want to have enough in twenty years, because in twenty years the cost of living will have driven up the prices of everything that you'll have to buy to live, and your insurance should reflect this increase in prices.

If you are willing to take the risk that you will become ill and become uninsurable, simply increase your protection each year or two by buying another policy. If you become ill and do not qualify, however, you'll not be able to do this and will forever be forced to carry a lesser amount of insurance than may be inadequate for your family.

PERMANENT INSURANCE: allows you to pay up the policy if you want and can afford to do so.

With permanent insurance, however, the premiums are higher than term insurance because of this benefit, which increases the risk to the insurance company and therefore costs you.

The premium on permanent insurance includes not only the cost of the risk of death (mortality risk), but also a "cash value" component. This means that if the premium is one hundred dollars but only $25 of that is for the mortality risk, the remaining $75 is cash value.

The cash value is eventually yours to keep if you decide to take it out of the policy. It therefore is a forced savings plan, something valuable to many people who would not otherwise save any money.

Permanent insurance comes in several sub-types: whole life, variable whole life, and universal life. The primary differences are shown below:

EFFECTS OF INFLATION

Dollars Invested	Rate of Inflation	Number of Years	Dollar Value After Inflation
$ 100	5%	5	78.35
100	5%	10	61.39
100	5%	15	48.10
100	5%	20	37.69
100	5%	25	29.53
100	7%	5	71.30
100	7%	10	50.84
100	7%	15	36.25
100	7%	20	25.84
100	7%	25	18.43
100	10%	5	62.09
100	10%	10	38.55
100	10%	15	23.94
100	10%	20	14.86
100	10%	25	9.23

* KEY: These figures clearly illustrate the loss of purchasing power you risk by not beating inflation over the long term.
**WHAT TO LEARN FROM THESE FACTS: It is not so important what kind of return you make from your savings and investments, but it *is* important that your return be better than inflation, in order to *protect your purchasing power.*

Type Death Benefit	Premium	Cash Values
Whole Life Fixed	Fixed	Guaranteed, at low interest rate
Variable	Fixed	Non-guaranteed
Whole Life	Fixed	Fixed non-guaranteed higher rate
Universal Life Flexible	Flexible	Non-guaranteed, at higher interest rate

NOTE: There are some variations on these kinds of insurance policies, but in general, these are the main categories, besides term insurance, to consider.

Your choice should depend on your need, your ability to pay premiums, and your health.

I strongly advise that you get objective financial advice before purchasing your insurance, as *this is the single most important purchase you will make in terms of providing security to your family in the event of death.*

Remember, you need from eight to twelve times your annual expenses to have adequate life insurance. If you own less protection than this, you need a very good reason to justify why.

SOCIAL SECURITY: IN THE EVENT OF DEATH

You may be saying to yourself, "Well, I don't need savings, or insurance, or investments, because if my spouse dies, I'll just collect his Social Security and live on that"... STOP HERE! You may not be eligible for Social Security!

Why? Because Social Security requires eligibility *before* you can collect on it. You are eligible if :

- you have at least forty "quarters" of employment (roughly ten years), or
- you are the spouse of an eligible employee, plus
- your spouse was already receiving Social Security retirement benefits, which you will receive as survivor beneficiary, and you are at least age sixty, or

- your spouse was not already receiving Social Security benefits, but you are at least sixty years of age, or
- your spouse was not already receiving Social Security benefits, but you are eligible because you are the caretaker parent of a dependent child under the age of eighteen, or you are disabled.

IN SUMMARY, you are not generally eligible for Social Security benefits of any kind, even as a survivor, until age sixty, unless you are either disabled or have minor children.

Now, in light of these rules, if you are counting on getting Social Security but are not eligible, you need to think again about starting a savings plan, an investment plan, and buying some life insurance.

GROUP INSURANCE: Sometimes an employer will provide group life insurance as part of your employee benefits. This is usually term insurance, except in less common cases of higher-paid executives and company owners.

Group term insurance on the rank-and-file employee is an employee benefit—it is issued based not on your age or health but on the size of the entire group of employees.

In addition, through the same policy or a companion policy, you can often purchase additional group insurance from your employer at a small cost. I recommend that you carry as much as is available to you through your employer. Keep in mind, however, that if you change jobs, you will lose this insurance. It is still a good benefit even if you have to pay a small premium for it, so take advantage of the inexpensive price and the guarantee of getting it whenever it is available through your employer.

INVESTMENTS: If the breadwinner dies, you should have enough insurance or enough investments to provide your family with the amount of income that they will need to survive at a normal standard of living.

To accomplish this with investments, they should be able to be converted to income if needed. By this I mean that you should be able to get a monthly check from your investments, to survive on them in lieu of the paycheck that your spouse had been bringing home. To find out what kinds of investments provide income and how, read chapter 9.

PENSION BENEFITS: If the breadwinner was in a company pension and was old enough to get retirement benefits, you as the surviving spouse may be entitled to those benefits. However, if the breadwinner was not old enough at the time of death to get benefits, you will usually have to wait until he would have been old enough. This means that if pension benefits are not payable until age fifty-five, and your spouse is fifty at the time of death, you will have to wait for five years, regardless of your own age, to get those pension benefits.

Sometimes, a pension plan includes a death benefit, payable to beneficiaries, in a lump sum. Sometimes this is in addition to monthly income but not always. It may be you can only get one or the other. If you are allowed to choose, often the lump sum is better, but not always, so *please get competent professional advice before selecting a lump sum over a monthly income, or vice versa.*

Congress has always mandated a lot of rules regarding pensions, but they are still somewhat varied, not uniform, making some of the provisions very different from one pension to another. You need to know exactly *what* your pensions provide, *how* to qualify for benefits, *when* you will get benefits, *what benefits choices* are available in the event of death, and *whom* to contact for help when needed.

I am constantly surprised by the number of people, usually women, who know nothing at all about the pension plans that their husbands have at work. I have been repeatedly asked to "find out if he had a pension" and "how much the pension is worth."

This, because until death, the wife in question never asked these questions, never knew the answers. Now, out of necessity, at a time of crisis, she is being forced to ask in order to survive. I think it is much better to know in advance, before a crisis occurs, and plan around the knowledge that you have.

Be realistic . . . even though most people do not die young, it can happen to anyone. Please don't allow yourself, or your spouse, to be so arrogant as to assume that you could never have happen to you what has already happened to thousands of other women when their young, healthy, active husbands die without warning!

WILLS: A will does not provide income, strictly speaking, but I mention it here anyway because it always comes into question at the time of death. A will determines what will happen to your estate when you die . . . who will get what and under what circumstances.

Without a will, the state in which you live will decide how to distribute your assets at death. In community-property states, the spouse is always the beneficiary and inherits virtually all assets except those that are not community property, UNLESS both spouses agree to otherwise.

WHAT IS COMMUNITY PROPERTY? It is everything that was acquired during the marriage, except an inheritance, a gift, or an asset purchased from the proceeds of an inheritance or gift, which asset was never titled in joint names with your spouse. In other words, if you inherited your mother's house at her death, during your marriage, but you never added your husband's name to the title of that house, it remains the separate property it was when you inherited it. However, if you changed the title by adding your husband's name, or put the money from the sale of the home in a joint bank account with your husband, it is community property even though it had originally been separate property.

Another example is that you inherit some money, and you and your husband jointly buy a boat with your inheritance. Now you have made your separate property into community property because you used the proceeds to buy the boat jointly. If you had bought the boat in your own name, separately, it would have remained separate, but when you "comingle" it, it becomes community property. "Comingled assets" are community assets.

Property or assets you owned prior to marriage are separate also, like inheritances or gifts, unless and until you likewise comingle them; then they, too, become community.

Most states in the United States are not community-property states. Instead, they are "common-law states." In common-law states, wives do not have a right to the income or assets of her husband in the same manner that she enjoys in a community-property state. In common-law states, a wife is not always the presumed beneficiary of all of the assets that her husband owns. The laws in each state vary, so while in a community-property state a wife is considered to be as much entitled to her husband's assets at death as she was during life, the same wife may not be entitled to her husband's assets if they lived in a common-law state at the time of his death. In this case, his children will be given a certain percentage of his assets, and she will be allocated a different share, not the entire estate.

This is why wills are so important. A will can override the provision in state law that would not give a wife the entire estate, or certain assets, or income.

In addition, wills specify who gets those little personal items and how the estate is to be handled and by whom.

Wills, if properly written, may specify how to get income from the assets named in the will. The will may name an investment advisor, a tax advisor, an attorney, or family representative to assist the family of the deceased at the time of death. The will may even set up a trust to take care of all of these details, sparing the beneficiaries and survivors from having to handle the details. Where both the husband and wife are normally intelligent, however, I do not advise trusts, as they are sometimes too restrictive, and they do cost money to manage yearly. Trusts work best when the primary beneficiary is aged, incompetent, very ill, a minor child, or institutionalized, but should not be presumed to be the answer for average people of normal intelligence. Trusts are also frequently used as a means of reducing estate taxes in a very large estate of over $1,200,000 net value at time of death.

A will should name the guardian and trustee for minor children of the deceased. Too many people fail to see the importance of this item, claiming that if the father dies, then the mother will naturally be the one to raise the children. However, what will happen if the mother and father both die, as in a car accident or a plane crash? Without wills, the court will decide who raises the children. I have seen grandparents fight in lengthy and bitter court battles to get custody of children simply because there were no wills. In addition, I have seen a few cases where the court awarded custody to someone other than the surviving parent, on the basis that there was no will and the surviving parent was unsuitable or unable to raise the children. I have also seen cases where one child went to one relative and another child went to another. *This is a sobering thought to most parents.*

SELLING THE FAMILY HOME: If you have a home, but no other assets, no pension benefits, no Social Security benefits (now), no insurance benefits, and cannot immediately earn a living, you will be forced to sell your home to survive financially at the death of your husband. This is not a pleasant thought, particularly since it is unlikely that the family home has enough equity to provide more than a few years of income. This is a real shame, in my opinion, when simple financial planning could routinely keep this from happening.

Nevertheless, it happens often. The average widow who is under age sixty at the time of the death of her husband will sell her home in less than three years because she needs the money on which to live, not because she no longer wants the family home.

If she is also raising children, she faces a bleak financial future as a result of this poor planning, because she will still need a place large enough to raise kids in, and her rent for a comparable place could end up as high or higher than the payment on the family home. In just a few years, her income from selling the home will run out and she will have nothing left to fall back on, having spent all of her assets for temporary income.

REMARRIAGE: While I know that some women would welcome remarriage, others declare that they would not. In fact, the statistics alone indicate that remarriage becomes rare for women over the age of forty, simply because of the small number of men age forty-and-over who are single. The fact is that single women over forty vastly outnumber single men over age forty, making remarriage statistically unlikely.

8

Getting Started with Investments

*B*efore you invest in anything, you need to learn some basic concepts in order to get started. These concepts arc called the *"basic principles of investing"* and are described next. *Be sure that you understand them before you start investing.*

THE BASIC PRINCIPLES OF INVESTING

1. Before you begin to invest money, be sure that you have saved up, in a savings account or money market fund, from three to six months' expenses. This means that if it takes two thousand dollars per month to pay your regular bills and buy food, you need to have saved up from six thousand dollars to twelve thousand dollars in cash, *before you start to invest in anything.*

Do not include luxuries or extras in your regularly monthly bills as part of this calculation; just count the necessities. *This money is for emergencies only*, to pay your bills if the breadwinner loses his job or becomes unable to work.

A recent example was from a client of mine who was employed by the airlines and got laid off from his job. He needed $1,300 per month to make their house payment, pay the utilities, pay the car insurance, buy gasoline, buy groceries, and pay property taxes. He had taken my advice and had saved up a little over nine thousand dollars cash. He ended up being out of work for a full six months but did not get into debt, or behind on their bills, as the nine thousand dollars was enough to get them by during that period of time.

2. Before you begin to invest money, carry adequate life insurance on the breadwinner. *If you cannot afford the amount of insurance you need, you cannot afford to invest.* Many people do not like to pay for life insurance, so they skip this step and go directly into investing. *Don't make this mistake!*

For example, each year I talk with a number of women who become widows unexpectedly. All are unprepared for the financial burdens that they face as a result. Even those whose husbands have a terminal illness tell me that they are unprepared. None has ever told me that her husband "had too much life insurance." In fact, I have found very few who had even *enough*. Most had to sell their homes, get a job, or live with relatives. With the cost of living in this country today, over 90 percent of the widows I have talked with have suffered financially because there was not enough life insurance on their husbands at the time of his death.

3. Establish a *reason* for investing. Make investing correspond to a purpose or goal. For example, you might set a goal of "investing for retirement," as many people do, or investing to pay off your mortgage early, or investing to accumulate for a future need, such as college, or travel, or income.

4. *Do not invest* for any goal that you want to meet in less than three years. Investments are long-term, not short-term; if you will need this money to meet a financial goal, or need, in less than three years, do not invest at all. Three years is not a long enough period of time for any investment. If you will need the money in three years or less, save the money in the bank or in a money market fund. Your invested money should be kept at work for much longer than three years.

5. *Become educated.* Read as much as possible about investing. Look for newer books that state that they explain concepts. (Read the introduction to find this out.) Also, start reading the financial pages and the business section of your newspaper even if you do not understand all that you read. Just read it all; eventually it *will* make sense. (Be patient.) In addition, attend seminars and classes (community colleges often offer investment classes and frequently gear them to women, in particular). Resist the temptation to invest as a result of any seminar you attend, as seminars sometimes do put a great deal of pressure on attendees to invest in a particular investment being explained. Just attend to *gather information,* to learn; say no to investments until you are truly ready and can afford them.

As an example, at every investment seminar or class that I give I am approached by someone who wants my opinion on an investment that she is considering. When I ask a few questions, most of these women reveal that they have not done their homework and are not prepared to make a good investment decision. Most want to invest out of sales pressure or greed and have done no planning at all. Most, therefore, are NOT ready to invest. The questions that I always ask, which will reveal to me whether or not a person is truly ready to invest, are: "Have you done a net worth statement and cash flow statement?" "Have you determined your tax bracket?" "Have you determined how much risk you can accept, and if so, what is that amount?" "Do you have adequate savings and life insurance already in place?" and "Do you have a written financial plan of some kind?" Most have done none of this but have a burning desire to invest in something that they are simply attracted to emotionally. Investments, however, should be bought and sold for gains, not because of emotions. *Leave your emotions at home when you begin to invest.*

6. Count up what you have already saved and make an outline of your general financial picture. You should have done your own financial statements (net worth and cash flow) as mentioned above and in chapter 2. You should have identified your financial strengths and weaknesses, with a plan for solving problems and reaching goals. If you have not already done this, stop here, go back, and do these things now.

7. Establish a relationship with a professional investment advisor. A Certified Financial Planner (CFP) will be your best resource for this relationship because a CFP is trained and educated to *teach* you as well as advise you. He or she will understand and encourage you to learn before investing and will usually spend a lot of time teaching you the kinds of things that you will need to know to invest wisely. Be prepared to pay the CFP for his or her time, as you are paying for the specialized knowledge that he or she has taken years to accumulate.

Typical fees charged by CFPs across the nation run from fifty dollars to $150 per hour, depending on the geographic area in which they live and practice. Big-city CFPs usually are more expensive than small-city CFPs.

8. Make up your mind that you will invest every month. The best way to do this is called "dollar cost averaging" (DCA), and it is the single best way to invest money, bar none. It reduces your risk and increases your profits for

some very good reasons that are, as usual, just common sense. Let me explain this concept of DCA in more detail.

DOLLAR COST AVERAGING (DCA)

This is buying shares in a mutual fund or stock (both of which are discussed and explained more in the next chapter) on a monthly basis, at a set dollar amount. For example, if you decide to invest one hundred dollars per month, every month, in a mutual fund, you would set it up to come out of your bank account on the same day each month, such as on the tenth, for exactly one hundred dollars. When you do this, you will be buying a different number of shares each month, at a different share price each time, because the prices of shares will change slightly from day to day.

FOR EXAMPLE:

One month, your hundred dollars may buy ten shares of XYZ Mutual Fund at ten dollars each share. The next month, your hundred dollars may buy 8.33 shares at twelve dollars each. The third month, the market falls, making share prices much lower, and your one hundred dollars buys twenty shares for five dollars each. After these three months, you end up with the following:

Month 1: 10.000 shares @ $10.00 each $100.00 total cash
Month 2:   8.333 shares @ $12.00 each $100.00 total cash
Month 3: 20.000 shares @ $5.00 each $100.00 total cash
          38.333 total shares * $300.00 total
*$300.00 total invested amount ÷ 38.333 shares
    = $ 7.83 average price per share.

Thus, instead of paying the higher prices per share, of ten or twelve dollars per share, by not buying all of your shares in one month, you were able to "average down" your price per share with the one month when share prices fell to five dollars. You ended up with an average price per share of only $7.83 instead of ten or twelve dollars. Keep in mind that you would not have been able to "average down" the price per share unless you had been buying *every* month.

WHY IS IT SO IMPORTANT TO "AVERAGE DOWN" THE SHARE PRICE?

The reason this is important is that when you sell your shares, say at retirement, you will make more profit from selling shares at fifteen dollars if you have an average price per share of $7.83, won't you, than if you had an average price per share of ten dollars or twelve dollars? Of course!

Simple math will illustrate this truth:

$ 15.00 price at retirement	$ 15.00 price at retirement
− *7.83 average purchase price*	− *10.00 average purchase price*
= $7.17 profit per share	= $5.00 profit per share
$7.17 profit per share is equal to a total return of 91.57 percent	$5.00 profit per share is equal to a total return of 50 percent

---

DOLLAR COST AVERAGING AS THE BEST METHOD OF INVESTING

Amount	Month	Share Price	# of Shares	Value
$250	1	$25	10.000	$250.00
250	2	27	9.259	519.99
250	3	24	10.417	712.22
250	4	19	13.158	813.85
250	5	14	17.857	849.67
250	6	15	16.667	1,160.37
250	7	14	18.857	1,347.01
250	8	17	14.706	1,885.66
250	9	16	15.625	2,024.74
250	10	21	11.905	2,907.47
250	11	22	11.364	3,295.93
250	12	20	11.500	3,246.40
3,000	1 YEAR	18.48	162.320	246.40
TOTAL		AVERAGE	SHARES	GAIN

*NOTE: the gain simply from dollar cost averaging = 8%. Remember that if the prices of shares did change, and stayed at 10% per share, you would have no gain.

**NOTE: not included in the above figures are the additional shares purchased with dividends in the automatic investment plan. These additional shares come to 21.583 shares. Valued at the final price of $20 per share, the additional shares increase the value of this account by $431.66, or an additional percentage of 14.389%, for a

TOTAL RETURN OF   22.389%

If you are investing, which would you prefer?

Do the math yourself and prove that DCA works! It is the most intelligent and least risky way to invest money over the long term, without exception! It is also the easiest way to invest.

Dollar cost averaging works only because the stock market *falls* from time to time. Do not believe that market crashes and declines in stock prices are all bad—this is not true.

HOW CAN YOU SAVE AND INVEST EVERY MONTH, *EASILY*?

The answer is that you can invest easily, every month, by a method called the "pre-authorized debit." This is a small form that you sign to allow your mutual fund to take a set amount of money out of your checking account each month, on the same day each month, to use to buy shares in your portfolio. Once you authorize this in writing, it will happen every month, until you change or cancel it. It is like a bill that gets paid every month, only it is paid to *you*, not to someone else. Most good mutual funds and many annuities will set this up for you as part of your account with them. Once you sign this form and give them a void check or deposit slip, they will do the rest of the work for you, and your monthly investment plan will go to work for you.

For example, I have many clients who want to invest in their IRA accounts by having $166 taken out of their checking accounts each month and deposited automatically into a mutual fund that they have set up for their IRAs. At the end of the year, their IRAs are already funded with two thousand dollars, easily and on a monthly basis.

9. Start small and increase the amount that you invest gradually. For example, after figuring out that your budget will allow you to invest twenty-five dollars per month, start with just that amount. If your budget will allow you to invest five hundred dollars per month, then start with that amount. Whatever amount your budget will allow is the amount that you should start your investment plan with, assuming you have done your homework in the other areas before you do invest. A year later, when you get a raise, use some of your raise to increase your monthly investment; all you have to do is complete a new "debit form," replace the old one with the new one, and send it to your mutual fund.

It is *amazing* how fast these small dollar amounts will grow! This is because the earnings "compound." *Compounding* means to pay earnings on top of earnings, which is why a small amount monthly can grow into a large amount over time.

To illustrate how compounding small amounts grow, consider: In only five years, $125 per month at 12% total return will grow to $10,672.78. In thirty years, that same amount at the same rate of growth will have grown to $405,438.91! It is sort of like the mustard seed that grows into a huge tree, isn't it?

10. Stick with your investments. Resist the temptation to sell them when the market gets bad, or when they have a bad year. All investments will have ups and downs, good years and bad years. Don't panic and bail out of an investment when the entire market is down, as it will eventually go back up. If you bail out when the market is down, you are guaranteed to lose money. If you wait until the market goes back up, you will not lose; and if you stay in until it goes up, you will gain.

Smart investors do not react much to the ups and downs in the market, and they don't panic everytime the market hiccoughs. As a result, history has proven time and time again that the smart investor is the patient investor and makes the most money with investments.

There is a saying: "Slow and steady wins the race." It is just as true in the investment field as in anything else. The patient investor will win in the long run, although it may not look that way when the market hops up and down.

11. Avoid "market timing." This is a fancy term for the so-called strategy of predicting what the stock market will do and moving your money around in anticipation of that. It requires that you hire a "market timer," a professional who specializes in this kind of work, to move your money for you; or you can do it yourself with a lot of sophisticated computer software. *The trouble is that it does not work.* It requires knowing *exactly* the right times to be "in the market" or "out of the market," and *no one has ever demonstrated an ability to know exactly when to do either of these things. It sounds great, but the trouble is that is just does not work.* All of their jumping in and out of the market has not given them any better profits than has simply buying shares and holding on to them for years. Market timers are only hoping for better results but have yet to actually get them. *Rule of thumb: Stay invested all of the time—*to

avoid the mistakes you will make if you try to guess which direction the market is going. You will not be able to guess correctly (no one ever has), so do not waste your time trying.

Let me tell you about a client of mine who invested some money in a couple of mutual funds in 1984. The funds did pretty well until October 19, 1987, when they fell by about 35 percent in value.

My client knew that this could happen and did not panic. In fact, she called me to ask if it would be a good idea to add some money to her funds. I agreed that it would, and she added one thousand dollars to each fund while it was down 35 percent in value. She bought shares for about "1/3 off," like a really good sale price on a quality dress. By January 1, 1988, less than three months later, her funds were back up, had completely recovered the 35 percent loss of October 19, and had even gained about 5 percent extra! By the middle of 1988, these same funds were up an additional 17 percent! This woman was not only patient—she went an extra step and made a great deal of money as a result!

12. *Diversify:* Don't put all of your eggs in one basket. *If you remember nothing else from this book, please remember this and the dollar cost averaging rule. Using these two rules will work better for you than anything else you try to use to make money by investing.*

This means don't buy just real estate, or just stocks, or just bank accounts, or just stock mutual funds. Mix it up. I have seen people with as much as five hundred thousand dollars invested in only five or six individual stocks. Instead, they should have been in five or six mutual funds, each of which invests in one hundred different stocks, so that their invested money is actually spread out to five hundred or six hundred different areas of risk. Investing in only five or six stocks, or only in real estate, is taking an incredible amount of risk with your money, and it is not necessary!

Why is this risky? Because if one of the five stocks becomes worthless, the investor has lost 20 percent of her portfolio. But if the investor had put the same money in five mutual funds, each with one hundred stocks, and the same stock had become worthless inside of the mutual fund, this same investor would have lost only .2%, less than a quarter of 1 percent of the total value. If one of the fifty stocks becomes worthless, the effect on the total portfolio is very small, and the chances are good that the other 499 stocks will easily offset the one bad stock. Not so with the undiversified portfolio of only five stocks; if one of them goes bad, it is *much* harder for the other four to make up the loss.

This is why diversification works as an investment strategy. It works with mutual funds, it works with real estate, it works with all kinds of investments. It is easy to accomplish this kind of diversification using mutual funds and annuities because it does not require a large amount of money to diversify with mutual funds and annuities. It does require larger amounts of money with real estate, but the principle is the same.

DIVERSIFICATION EXAMPLE

John and Mary put $100,000 into a bank CD, guaranteed to pay 8% for 20 years. Mike and Debbie, however, decide to take some risk, and after carefully studying their choices with a professional financial advisor, they put $20,000 into 5 different investments for 20 years, none guaranteed to pay any rate of return. **What are the results?**

	Initial Investment	Annual Return	Value After 20 Years
John and Mary:	$100,000	8%	$466,096
Mike and Debbie:	$ 20,000	total loss	–0–
	20,000	0%	20,000
	20,000	5%	53,066
	20,000	10%	134,550
	20,000	15%	<u>327,331</u>
			$534,947

Mike and Debbie end up with $68,851 more!

Diversification cuts losses and increases returns.
DIVERSIFY ! !

---

13. *Reinvest all of your earnings.* By this, I mean that you should not spend any of the earnings that you make from investing. Let these earnings be added to your account so that it can grow and grow and grow. You can easily do this by simply marking a small box on the form you fill out to open your account. That is all that there is to it; the mutual fund or annuity company will reinvest your earnings automatically for you.

The way that this happens is that every time your fund earns interest, dividends, or a capital gain, the fund itself will automatically reinvest it in more shares in the fund. This is called "automatic reinvestment" or "systematic reinvestment." As your number of shares grows, with the passage of time, these shares will grow in value as well as number. You will be amazed to see how your portfolio grows in value without any effort on your part. All you need to do is keep adding to the mutual fund or annuity and be patient.

INVESTMENTS HAVE RISK. How do you invest without putting your money at too much risk? That is a very good question, as all investments have some degree of risk. Anyone who tells you that there is no risk in a particular investment is lying or mistaken.

WHAT KINDS OF RISKS EXIST?

There is the risk that you might not get a very good return, or that you might be in the right investment but at the wrong time, or that all investments of that type might have a bad year overall, or that you might even lose your money.

A greater risk, however, is that you will not invest at all, because you do not want to take any risk. People do this when they are so afraid of all risk that they never get the courage to invest at all. *When this happens, you are absolutely guaranteed to lose money—to inflation.*

Inflation robs more people than any other kind of risk. It is absolutely guaranteed to deplete your wallet, your bank account, and your savings, and it never stops stealing from your pocket. WHY? Because inflation represents a *"loss of purchasing power."*

To understand what this means, remember where I said earlier in this book that there are only a few things that you can do with money, one of which is to spend it. Well, what you spend in twenty years on food and electricity will be more than what you spend today on the same items . . . because prices keep going up. The house that cost fourteen thousand dollars in 1962 sold for $185,000 in 1991. Gasoline that you bought for twenty-five cents in 1960 osts $1.21 in 1994. Beef that cost sixty-nine cents a pound in 1971 runs $1.79 per pound in 1993. *This is inflation . . . and it robs you of your purchasing power, one of your most important reasons for having money at all.*

If your purchasing power declines, so does the value of whatever money you have. If you can't buy as much with your money, it is not as valuable. To protect yourself against inflation, *your money must grow in value*. To accomplish this goal, your money, through investments, must earn more than the rate of inflation. If inflation averages 6 percent for the next ten years, you MUST get more than 6 percent on your investments, on average, to keep pace. *Inflation is the greatest risk you face and beating it should be your #1 long-term goal.*

Most people are simply too conservative, usually because they do not understand investing well enough to take responsible risks. They do not feel "secure" with investing.

Most will go to their bank and deposit their investment dollars. But this is not true investing—it is saving, which is good up to a point but should not be confused with true investing at all.

Here is a classic example of being too conservative: There were two investors. The first "did not want to take any risk" and put all of her money in the bank, where it was "guaranteed" (only the interest rate was guaranteed). The second investor was willing to take some risks and knew that she would reduce her risks by diversifying, so she put her money in five different mutual funds. The results are shown below. As you can see, they are dramatic!

Investor #1	**Investor #2**
Invested one hundred thousand dollars in the bank for twenty years	Invested twenty thousand dollars in five mutual funds
Got 8% annual return each year for twenty years	Lost all her money in one investment
Had no losses	Made 0% on the 2nd investment
	Made 5% on the 3rd investment
	Made 10% on the 4th investment
	Made 15% on the 5th investment
Ended up with $466,096	Ended up with $534,947

That's a difference of *$68,851*!
What does this tell you about *risk*?

To summarize investment risks, keep in mind that while there are a number of real risks associated with investing, you can avoid many of them by diversifying your money into several areas. If you have only a little bit of money with which to do this, you can accomplish it by using mutual funds. Even if you have plenty of money, you can and should be using mutual funds for diversification.

If you choose good investments, meaning good quality, and most of them do well, you will have great success in investing.

One of the most successful investors of all time, John Templeton, founder of the well-known and highly respected Templeton Funds, a professional investment manager with over forty-five years of experience, has stated that *it is only necessary to be right 60 percent of the time to obtain better than average investment results over the long term.* Mr. Templeton is correct. So *losses are to be expected* and are part of the norm, but if you diversify, some of your investments will more than make up for your losses and will even be the reason for the overall better-than-average profits, certainly better than if you kept your money "invested" in the bank, where it was "safe."

So, do not be afraid of risk but understand that risk can be managed and know what kinds of risks you will be taking. This is where a good professional financial planner will help you. He or she will outline all of the risks and help you make good investment decisions that match your needs and your goals.

A financial planner will also help you get started with good investments in many cases. He or she can explain each kind of investment and tell you why one or several are better suited to you than others. You will become more and more educated as you ask more and more questions, read, and begin to invest your own money. This is how you get started, and it is never too early to do it.

INVESTING SUMMARY

Once you decide to become an investor and have an investment goal, you must get started. It is okay to start small. In fact, I recommend it.

Make your investment dollars part of your monthly budget. Set up an automatic investment plan and invest a set dollar amount every month, through a DCA plan.

Reinvest all of your earnings. Do not spend any of them and use mutual funds to accomplish this reinvestment plan.

Stick with your investments for the long term and do not pay too much attention to the ups and downs of the market. Market swings are normal.

Remember the big keys: DCA, diversification, and patience!

In 1984 I advised a young couple who will serve as a good example of good investing. They had been married only four years, had one child, and were living in a mobile home on ten acres that they were buying. They were serious about getting started on an investment plan, had a goal of investing fifty dollars per month, had good insurance on both of them, and had saved up four thousand dollars in cash.

Today (1994) they have three children, a prosperous small business, a beautiful home worth $225,000 on five acres with only a $55,000 mortgage on it, a renter living in their mobile home, and $48,398 invested in mutual funds from a fifty dollars per month investment plan.

You, too, can start small and be successful, but you have to stop wishing and wanting and get started.

TYPES OF INVESTMENTS

*T*o begin, I want to simplify the confusion by letting you know a little-known fact: There are actually only *four basic types of investments,* even though you hear countless different names for and references to investments. Most of the names that you hear are only "labels," designer labels in some cases but *not* really a new category of investment.

These four categories of investments are:

1. Debt investments
2. Equity investments
3. Natural resources
4. Business

Let me briefly describe and explain each category, starting with the most common and most familiar to the majority of people. *This category of investment is debt.*

DEBT INVESTMENTS: A debt investment is a bank account at a bank, credit union, or savings and loan, a bond, an annuity, an insurance policy, a certificate of deposit from a bank, credit union, or savings and loan, a government security such as a Treasury bill (a "T-bill"), a Treasury bond or note, or a contract that you accept when you sell any asset.

"Investing in debt" means that you have lent your money to someone, some company, or the U.S. government, in return for interest. At the end of a certain period of time, you are supposed to get your original money back, except with a contract, which is explained last.

#1.
DEBT: This is the most commonly used type of investment in the U.S. It consists of:
- bank accounts
- life insurance
- annuities
- corporate bonds
- government bonds
- real estate contracts
- certificates of deposit
- other interest-bearing investment

From low risk to high risk. All types and categories. Speculative to very conservative.

#2.
REAL ESTATE: Another common form of investment in the U.S. It may be a home, or a rental property, or piece of real estate owned by a partnership. You may own it entirely or as a part-owner with other people. It may be paid for or you may have a mortgage on it.

Moderate to high risk. All real estate subject to higher degrees of risk than debt and equity investments. Lower risk than nat. res.

#3.
EQUITY: This usually is going to refer to stocks. Stocks are the most common form of equity, which is another word for "ownership." To "have equity" in an investment is to own it, fully or partially. Owning stock means that you have equity in a corporation, and own shares, which represent all or part of the shares of that corporation. The "Equity market" refers to the stock market.

From low risk to high risk. Conservative to speculative. All categories/types.

#4.
NATURAL RESOURCES: These are those resources that are found in nature. Most are able to be renewed, like farm crops, timber, fish and game, animals raised for food or by-products, gold, silver, and industrial metals, diamonds and other gems, oil, gas, and petroleum by-products, and other resources that make life possible and are bought and sold for their basic investment potential.

Speculative and high risk.

A rule of thumb is to balance a porfolio between these four basic categories of investment. Most people consider their home as the largest investment, in the 2nd category, then Debt, in #1, and then, if at all, they invest in #3, Equity. They would be better off in #3, Equity, as their first investment, then #2, then #1, Debt, in that order. Most people never use #4.

If you lend money, you have therefore invested in debt as your investment. It is not your own debt; it is someone else's debt. You receive a certain percentage of interest paid to you, for a specific period of time, and at the "maturity" of your investment you get your principal back. *This is what banks, credit unions, and savings and loans do all of the time.* They lend money to people and make money on the interest they charge.

When you open a bank account or purchase a certificate of deposit, you have "*lent*" your money to that bank. If you open a savings account that you can close at any time, you have opened what is called a "demand deposit" account. It means that you can go into the bank at any time and demand your deposit back with whatever interest that you are entitled to receive. Because the bank has no assurance that you won't do exactly that, tomorrow, they will pay you a lower rate of interest on this money you are lending to them.

If, however, you will promise to keep your money on deposit for a certain period of time, such as twelve months, the bank will pay you a higher rate of interest because they can count on this money's staying with them for at least that long.

In the meantime, they lend out your money, which you have lent to them, and they charge even higher interest to the person to whom they lend your money. *This is the banking business in a nutshell.*

All debt investments work this way, whether you lend your money to the bank, or to a corporation by buying a corporate bond, or to the government by buying a government bond or Treasury bill, or on a contract that represents something you are selling to a buyer whom you allow to pay you back gradually, in payments. *All of these kinds of investments represent debt investments.*

EQUITY INVESTMENTS: *Equity means "ownership."* If you *"have equity"* in something, you have *ownership* in it. If your equity is one hundred percent, you own *all* of it. If your equity is fifty percent, you own fifty percent of it. If your equity is ten percent, you own ten percent of it.

An easily understandable example of equity is in owning a house. If you owe fifty thousand dollars on a house that is worth one hundred thousand dollars, you have a 50 percent equity, or ownership, in that house. As you gradually pay down the mortgage, or as the value of the house increases, your equity increases.

For example, on the same house, if you owe fifty thousand dollars but it increases in value to one hundred fifty thousand dollars, your equity is now 67 percent instead of 50 percent, just because the value of the house has increased. On the other hand, if you owe fifty thousand dollars on your house and it declines in value to seventy-five thousand dollars, your equity is now only 33 ⅓ percent.

Stocks are commonly referred to as *"equities."* This is so because stocks represent the broadest form of ownership in a corporation, and thus, in *"corporate America." Stock ownership is the most basic form of capitalism that exists, along with land ownership.* When you own stock, you own a small part (or maybe a large part if you own a lot of the stock of that corporation) of that company.

When you buy stock on the stock market, you are buying a small piece of the corporations represented by the stocks you purchase. For example, if you buy one hundred shares of Boeing Corporation, you own a small (very small) part of Boeing itself. The larger the company, the smaller your share of ownership, but it is ownership nevertheless. *It is not debt.*

Owners usually get to vote as a result of owning shares, as well. Your vote may or may not count much, especially if you only own a very small part of the company, but you generally do get the right to vote. Your shares are thus generally referred to as "voting shares."

The more voting shares you own, the greater your ability to control the corporation. That is why some people, or other corporations, like to buy a majority interest in the voting shares of another corporation, not just to have ownership but also to control how the company is run. Ultimately, the buyer of a majority of shares may be trying to take over entirely, which is sometimes referred to as a "hostile takeover attempt." Profit is the usual motive for this kind of takeover attempt.

When the term *equities* is used, it therefore refers more often than not to stocks. It is also referred to in describing the degree of ownership you have in any particular piece of real estate. *The key to remember is that equity refers to ownership, while debt refers to lending money.*

I have a preference for equity as an investment. My preference may be viewed by some as a bias, but there is good reason that I prefer equity over other types of investments.

This is because equities, over the long term, tend to do better than other types of investments.

Taking inflation into consideration, it makes sense that equity investments will protect an investor better over the long term than will debt investments. There is a place for debt investments in most people's lives and portfolios, more so as they get older, but *debt should not represent the greatest part of any portfolio for long periods of time*. Debt is okay when interest rates are temporarily high, but not for the long, long term. Equity investments have historically yielded about 4 percent to 5 percent more per year, on average, than debt investments.

Put another way, the stock market has done better over time than the bond market, certificates of deposit, annuities, and government securities (T-bills, and so forth) by about 4 percent or 5 percent per year, on average. These are *real* numbers, too, not manipulated numbers. Specifically, the average long-term compounded annual total return of equity investments versus debt investments, from 1925 to 1988, has been:*

U.S. Treasury bills 3.1 %
Inflation 3.5%
Long-term government bonds 4.4%
Common stocks (all U.S. companies) 10.0%
Common stocks (small U.S. companies) 12.3%
*Source: Ibbotson & Associates

So, stocks (equities) of U.S. corporations, did much better over a very long period than both debt investments and inflation, as shown by history.

This same result can be shown to happen over much shorter periods of time, such as ten years and twenty years, too. It is a normal phenomenon that stocks do better over periods of at least ten years than other investments, despite the losses that stocks sometimes experience and despite the swings in the stock market.

Since true investors should only invest for the long term, rather than short term, *this is a very important piece of information to have*. This historical data tells me and most savvy investors that equities are better over the longer term and will probably outperform inflation as well as other investments. *With inflation being your biggest risk, this is good news for any investor.*

TYPES OF STOCK: There are several different types of stocks. There are "preferred stocks" and "common stocks." But first you need to understand some of the basics of all stocks before looking at the differences between these two kinds of stocks.

Since stocks represent ownership in a corporation, they can be bought and sold easily. This is what happens daily on the stock markets all over the world, including New York.

There are stock markets in New York, Tokyo, London, Germany, Canada, other parts of Asia, other parts of Europe, and in the Middle East and South America. There are also several independent stock markets in the United States, referred to commonly as the "broad market" and the "over-the-counter market," meaning not the New York Stock Exchange in New York City (Wall Street).

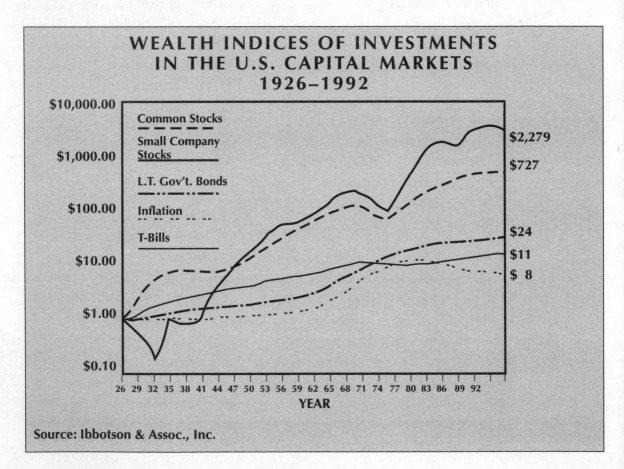

WEALTH INDICES OF INVESTMENTS IN THE U.S. CAPITAL MARKETS 1926–1992

Common Stocks
Small Company Stocks
L.T. Gov't. Bonds
Inflation
T-Bills

$2,279
$727
$24
$11
$ 8

YEAR

Source: Ibbotson & Assoc., Inc.

Many Americans buy and sell in these foreign stock markets, *which by the way, make up about 75% of the total stocks in the entire world. The U.S. stock market only accounts for 25% of the activity of buying and selling stocks around the world.* We are really only a small, minority part of the bigger global stock market. My guess is that Europe will eventually, probably soon, emerge as the biggest stock market in the world. This is part of their economic unification plan, and they are well on their way to achieving this.

LONG-TERM INVESTING: RESULTS

Dollar Amt. Invested Monthly	Number of Years	Total Return %	Value of Dollars Invested	
$ 250	5	8	19,007.79	
$ 250	5	10	20,146.83	+ 2,400!
$ 250	5	12	21,345.57	
$ 250	10	8	46,936.46	
$ 250	10	10	52,593.50	4% better yield =
$ 250	10	12	58,963.75	26% more!
$ 250	15	8	87,972.85	
$ 250	15	10	104,849.19	
$ 250	15	12	125,259.84	
$ 250	20	8	148,268.76	
$ 250	20	10	189,007.50	
$ 250	20	12	242,096.21	
$ 250	25	8	236,863.25	
$ 250	25	10	324,545.30	almost double!
$ 250	25	12	448,007.80	

* NOTE the difference between the amounts accumulated in 25 years, comparing an 8% total return to a 12% total return; there is almost twice as much ($211,138.55) accumulated as a result of getting 4% more in total return on your money over the years. This is due largely to the long-term effects of compounding of earnings, and reinforces the need to reinvest all earnings, rather than spending them.

Stocks earn dividends. A dividend is a share of the profits of a corporation. It is paid "per share" of stock. It is usually about 3 percent or 4 percent on average and is paid to the owner of the stocks, called the shareholder, quarterly in most cases.

The dividend is not guaranteed or fixed. The board of directors of the corporation meets quarterly and reviews the profitability of the company and "declares the dividend" based on how profitable the company has been during the previous quarter. If the company has not been profitable, it may not declare a dividend. If it has been profitable, the board will probably declare a dividend. Sometimes a board of directors will skip the payment of dividends in order to "retire debt."

This means that they feel that the company, just like people, has too much debt and wishes to use some of the profits to pay off some or all of the offending debt. This is often wise, as corporations can get into trouble over debt just as people can do. Sometimes a board will skip paying dividends to invest in "capital improvements" also, which means to buy or replace equipment or do something like this to improve the company and make it more profitable in the future. Corporations need to do this from time to time, and sometimes they do use profits that would otherwise be paid out as dividends for this purpose. Some do not, however. Your job as an investor will be to learn the dividend-paying history of any stock you are considering buying, so that you know whether or not to buy on that basis.

Dividends are paid only to the owner of the shares of stock. There are two kinds of owners, just as there are two kinds of stock: preferred shareholders and common shareholders. The kind of shareholder you *are* depends on the kind of stock you *own*.

Preferred stocks are those that are paid a dividend *first,* out of whatever profits are available. Then, after the preferred shareholders are paid their dividends, the common shareholders are next paid their dividend. If there is only enough profit to pay the preferred shareholders, the common shareholders may not receive a dividend.

Preferred shares generally do not fluctuate much in value as do common shares. They are not usually bought and sold as much as common stock, either. People who own preferred shares tend to hang on to them for very long periods of time. Some companies do not even issue preferred shares; many issue only common shares.

While common shares are generally a little bit more risky than preferred shares, they also usually grow more in value, and much faster, than preferred shares. The majority of investors buy common shares rather than preferred shares for this reason.

I generally do not advise or recommend preferred shares as an investment, unless the investor is extremely conservative, such as a trust account or a very elderly individual with enough income not to be too concerned about inflation for the next few years. Otherwise, I am concerned about inflation and will usually recommend and advise investors to buy common stocks. However, I do it in the form of mutual funds rather than in individual stocks. Read on to learn why.

MUTUAL FUNDS: *Mutual funds are by far my favorite type of investments, suitable for virtually all investors.*

A mutual fund is the common term for what is known in the investment industry as a "regulated investment company." It is a professional firm that does nothing except invest money in stocks and bonds for people who are investor clients.

Most mutual fund clients are individuals, just like you and me. Some are corporations, some are pension funds, some are trusts, and some are wealthy individuals, but the vast majority are simply ordinary people of average incomes and means.

A mutual fund is managed by investment professionals who research corporations, governments, government agencies, the economy, the stock and bond markets, and worldwide events continuously. These professionals have specialty expertise in every conceivable type of business, government, and industry imaginable. Some specialize in the transportation industry, while others specialize in the apparel industry, while others may be particularly expert in the oil business, while still others might be quite expert in just the child care industry, and so on.

These professionals also study and understand (as much as humanly possible!) the stock and bond markets worldwide.

They watch the emotional swings, the mood of investors in general, the "psychology of the market," and the swings that occur in the markets from day to day. They want to know if investors feel confident, or optimistic, or pessimistic.

For example, after the Persian Gulf War many investors were feeling very positive, and this drove the stock market up in value. Mutual fund professionals *watch* these things closely in order to uncover opportunities for investing in which to make money and to avoid problem areas of the market.

Mutual funds are usually managed by an individual or a team, with a specific person in charge of the decision to buy or sell any particular stock or bond. There are frequently twenty or thirty people behind this manager, doing research, traveling to visit the companies being considered, examining the financial records of the companies, and watching the trends in the economy and the markets.

When the fund manager makes the decision to buy or sell a stock, he or she also determines the right price for this buying or selling. It is a very practical decision, never based on emotion. The manager simply makes the decision and waits until the right time to execute his or her decision. If the "right time" never comes, the manager generally does nothing. *It is strictly business, thank you.*

On the other hand, most individuals who attempt to buy and sell stocks tend to get quite emotional about it. This does not work out very well in most cases, as individuals are just not trained, experienced, or equipped to make the kinds of investment decisions that are necessary to successfully invest in the stock and bond market. Individuals also do not generally have the time to do the kind of research required to make informed investment decisions, nor do they have access to the data that is definitely needed to make good investment decisions. Mutual funds do, which is why they are a better choice than investing in individual stocks and bonds.

When you invest in a mutual fund, which you can do for as little as twenty-five dollars per month in some funds (others may require much higher amounts), you deposit your cash into the fund. They open an account for you in your name, in an account number that is your own.

You will receive statements on your account regularly. Instead of your account's showing the value of your investment in dollars, however, it will show the value in shares. The more shares you own, the more profits you will enjoy.

This is because your mutual fund represents a portfolio of stocks or bonds, or both, selected by your fund, in as many as one hundred different companies/government issues. The mutual fund owns these investments in a portfolio and gives you a share of that portfolio.

To do this, they issue shares to you, just like shares in a corporation. If and when the value of the shares in their portfolio goes up, so do your shares in the mutual fund as well. IF the value of the portfolio goes down, the value of your shares of that portfolio also goes down. Fluctuations in share prices of any mutual fund are to be expected.

Over time, mutual funds, especially the better ones, have done better even than stocks as well as all other types of investments. The reason is that the kind of professional management that mutual funds offer is truly superior in general. *There are, of course, good mutual funds and bad mutual funds, but overall, they have been the best kind of long-term investment available to investors.*

Mutual funds earn their yield from the interest paid on the bonds in the portfolio and from the dividends paid on the stocks in the portfolio. They add these together when they receive them and then pay them to the investors that own shares of the fund—you. However, that is not the only way they earn for you.

In addition, if the stocks and bonds go up in value, the fund manager will often decide to sell them for a profit. When this is done, the profit is referred to as a "capital gain," and this additional money is also paid to the investors who own shares in the mutual fund.

All of these earnings, when combined together, are referred to as the "total return." Total return never refers only to the interest or the dividends earned; these are the sources of the "current yield." The total return is *everything combined*.

Sometimes, if the market is bad, or declines, as it did in October 1987 (and many times prior to 1987), the value of your shares in the mutual fund will decline also. This is not a cause for major concern, generally.

Most mutual funds, *including* the really good ones, will experience times when their shares *will* decline in value. This happens on a cyclical basis, over and over again. The key to remember is that when the market has gone down, it has always gone back up again. The shares of a good mutual fund tend to follow this up-and-down cycle.

What does "the market is down" actually mean?

This means that the prices of stocks have fallen. This happens all of the time. They decline in value. But, they also often go up in value, too. Sometimes stock prices rise or fall because the entire market (all stocks and all bonds) are either rising or falling in value. Other times only certain stocks are rising, or falling, or just a particular industry of stocks, such as automobile stocks. Sometimes only a segment of the larger U.S. economy is in decline, so the stocks in that segment will be down, or up, as the case may be.

When you hear that the "market is down" by thirteen points, this simply refers to the fact that a certain number of stocks has declined in price, for that one day. It does not refer to all stocks. Generally, this is reported as the "Dow-Jones quote," or the "New York quote," or the "over-the-counter quote" or the "broad market quote."

Sometimes you hear about the "Dow-Jones Industrial average," which sounds pretty important, but it is actually only fifty specific stocks of major U.S. industries, big companies quoted to reflect the condition of the entire market. *In fact, however, the Dow-Jones Industrial average is no longer a good measure of the entire market, as the market and the worldwide economy, particularly the U.S. economy, is moving out of being an industrial economy into a service and information economy.* So, the fifty stocks in the Dow-Jones Industrial average are less of an indicator of this new service and information economy than they used to be.

Stocks not listed (offered) on the New York Stock Exchange are mostly traded (bought and sold) on a bigger market, called the "broad market." Some of these "broad market" stocks are listed somewhere on a smaller exchange (instead of New York) and sometimes they are just sold through a computer system that tracks all stocks, regardless of where they are listed.

From time to time, certain types of business in any economy will experience a decline in profits, productivity, and employment. These are called "cyclical industries." The cycles that these industries go through are somewhat predictable. Usually they are temporary and do not indicate that the particular business is in financial trouble that they cannot survive. When this happens, the businesses in these industries are often referred to as being "out of favor." You see, investors too often want only to invest in companies that are "in favor," or fashionable, or obviously profitable, and these same investors can overlook the chance to purchase good stocks, at bargain prices, in solid companies that are only temporarily out of favor. Sometimes these companies are excellent stocks to buy, precisely because they are out of favor with the majority of investors.

In fact, a good rule of thumb for a *savvy, professional investor* is that if the majority of individual investors *likes* a particular company and is buying a lot of it, that is the time to *sell* your shares, but when the majority does not like a company, that is the time to *buy* (assuming it is a good company to begin with) as it is out of favor and hence a great buy. This is commonly referred to as the "contrarian theory" and is exactly how most fortunes are made in stocks and bonds. *The logic behind this is that in investments, the crowd is generally wrong, so you should not follow the crowd. It's a lot like life, as a matter of fact.*

At times, due to war, pessimism overseas, a recession, or pessimism at home, the market experiences a decline in general. When this happens, most stock prices fall. This is not usually an indication that there is serious financial trouble with any particular company. It is more of an indicator of a bad economy than a bad stock.

More often than not, the price of a stock (or bond) will rise and fall because of the supply-and-demand situation. It is just common sense; when an item is in strong demand, the price for that item frequently goes *up*. If it is *not* in strong demand, the seller will "*put that item on sale*" (the price will go *down*) because he has to do so in order to sell it at all, and he has to sell it in order to *survive*.

Buyers and sellers of stocks and bonds are not much different from buyers and sellers of dresses, foods, cars, or houses. They want the best price they can get, but the price they get more often than not depends greatly on the demand and the supply of whatever they have to sell.

This buying and selling of stocks and bonds is called "trading." There are special experts, at the New York Stock Exchange (and other places), who do nothing but "trade" stocks and bonds, mostly for other people, but also for themselves or for brokerage firms. It is quite an interesting fact, a little-known fact, that most traders do not make a profit on their trades overall, even though they might make a profit on a particular day. Studies seem to show that traders lose more often than they gain. If this is true, one would wonder why they do what they do. That is a reasonable question, and there is a logical answer. The answer is that they earn a commission on each trade, regardless of whether the trade is at a loss or a profit. The broker always gets paid, no matter whether the investor makes any money or not.

So the markets are sometimes driven by trading, and other times by profits, and other times by greed, and other times by fear. You get the picture by now, I imagine. It is a fascinating game with a little bit of logic, a lot of psychology, and a lot more research. A smart investor buys and sells strictly on the logic and research available to him or her. Most of us need to take advantage of the expertise in mutual funds to be able to really accomplish just that.

TYPES OF MUTUAL FUNDS

Equity Funds—stock funds in the following categories:

Small companies
Specialty industries (utilities, high tech, precious metals, health care, banking, and so forth)
International companies
Growth companies (businesses that get bigger and have lots of room to grow)
Aggressive growth companies (companies getting bigger very quickly)

Hybrid Funds—mixed funds in the following categories:

Asset allocation funds (selected market segments)
Balanced funds (a balanced mix, i.e., 50% stocks and 50% bonds)
Income funds (funds that pay income from dividends and interest)
Junk bond funds (cheaper, poorer quality bonds)
Index funds (market averages, all categories)

Fixed Income Funds—in the following categories:
Bond funds (corporate and U.S. government bonds)
International bond funds (bonds of foreign governments)
Municipal bond funds (tax-exempt bonds of municipal governments, i.e., cities)
Money market funds (cash funds, with checking account privileges)

Please remember that mutual funds come in many sizes, types, and styles. You can buy mutual funds that specialize in stocks only, or bonds only, or a mix of stocks and bonds. Some funds invest only in government securities such as Treasury bills, Treasury notes, or bonds. Other funds invest only in municipal bonds, while still others only invest in small corporations.

Now, you can even select a mutual fund that specializes in stocks of companies, in the United States and overseas, which meet environmental or social standards. These funds are called "socially responsible funds" and tend to avoid investing in companies that have track records of treating their employees badly, of being involved in the production of alcohol, tobacco, or weapons, or they might avoid companies that pollute.

Instead, they seek out companies that make a business of observing certain human-rights standards and that clean up the environment. These funds appeal to the investor that does not want to invest in what *they* consider morally or socially irresponsible businesses.

These kinds of funds are gaining in popularity *very* fast. At the same time, some are proving to be good investments, as it seems that cleaning up the environment is big business, indeed, and quite profitable.

Most mutual funds have clearly defined objectives. One might have as its objective, or goal, to produce income, while another might have as its goal the "appreciation of capital." The first objective is self-explanatory: It intends to invest in whatever it can find that will provide steady income to the investors who invest in that fund. Appreciation of capital simply means to "grow in value." Since a mutual fund is a financial firm, the capital being referred to is money, so a fund that wants appreciation of capital merely wants to grow the value of the money invested through appreciation of the companies it owns. When you invest in something that grows in value, your dollars invested tend to do much better than if they are simply earning interest. This can be easily seen when you consider why most people feel comfortable buying a house. Including the ability to have a place in which to live, most people hope that the value of their house will go up, and most people expect this to happen. They want the house to appreciate. When it does, the money they have paid for the house is money invested wisely, because their investment and their money invested grows in value.

Mutual funds have the same goal and the same expectations when they buy stock in various companies. They hope for an increase in value, for appreciation of capital.

In fact, stocks as a category of investment have, indeed, appreciated in value over the years, as much or more than real estate. And stocks have far outperformed inflation; they have appreciated in value at a rate much greater than the average annual rate of inflation. The result is that dollars that were invested in stocks have ended up being worth more over time, after inflation, than all other types of investments, many of which only barely kept up with inflation.

ADVANTAGES OF MUTUAL FUNDS

- **Professional Management**
- **Diversification**
- **Automatic Reinvestment**
- **Liquidity**
- **Systematic Withdrawals**
- **Regular Reporting**

HOW DO MUTUAL FUNDS MAKE MONEY FROM YOUR MONEY?

They do so in several ways. First, they all charge an internal fee called a "management fee." It is the cost of letting them manage the fund, a fee well worth paying. It is usually very small and comes out of the yield that the fund makes. It gives the fund management a powerful incentive to make money, for you and for them. A typical management fee might be .45%, or less than a half of one percent. Other funds have higher fees, usually for good reasons, such as a portfolio that is more complicated, more difficult to manage.

Mutual funds sometimes also make money from another fee, called a "load." A load is a commission paid to a salesperson who sells the fund. Loads can range from 2% to 8% and there are some even higher. The investor can pay one of three kinds of loads: a "front-load" that is paid out of the amount invested, or a "back-load" paid out of the value of the account when it is closed (prior to a certain date, sometimes), or "12-b–1 fees," a type of load that is ongoing and can range from .15% to .25% annually.

A load is charged on mutual funds that employ a sales force rather than by funds who sell their shares through advertising or direct mail. The job of the sales force is to explain the fund, do the paperwork, and provide ongoing service to the investor.

Sometimes this is very valuable and worth the money spent on the load. Sometimes it is not. If you buy a fund and pay a load, you should expect personal service and stay in touch with the agent who sold you the fund, at least for a few years.

Some funds are called "no-load" funds. They charge no load to buy or sell shares. They have no salespeople to explain the fund, and they rely on advertising to let you know about themselves. They often require larger initial investment amounts as well, compared to the load funds, who will take very small amounts of money and smaller monthly amounts on a DCA plan. There are also no-load funds that are available only to "institutional investors" such as pension funds; they are not available to the general public at all.

What is really important, regardless of the fees charged, is the total return, (net of fees paid) to the investor, over a certain period of time, preferably 10+ years. These total returns are calculated and published routinely by companies that track mutual funds and rate the many mutual funds available.

Today there are about 6000 mutual funds in existence in the United States alone. One of these companies that tracks mutual funds and is widely recognized as reputable and accurate is a company called *Morningstar Publications*. It publishes a periodical called *Mutual Fund Values,* a rating of all mutual funds in the United States. This periodical is arranged as a journal, with new editions published every two weeks. It rates, explains, compares, and summarizes almost all mutual funds. You can read it at any large public library. I recommend a beginner investor do exactly that.

A competent certified financial planner (CFP) will have *Mutual Fund Values* available *also* and maybe some additional resources and services to rate mutual funds. In this way, it is fairly easy to find out which are the best funds, a question you have probably already asked as you read this chapter.

These track records have been kept for many years and explain what kind of fund each fund is, who manages the fund, what the specific objectives are for the fund, the degree of risk associated with the fund, what companies the fund invests in, peculiarities of the fund, how the fund compares to other funds, and the overall rating (on a 1–5 star system, like that of restaurants and hotels).

Careful study of a mutual fund, before buying, with the help of a good CFP, is well worth the effort, time, and money spent on advice. My own experience has been that most individuals do not have access to enough information to successfully pick the right mutual fund for their own situation, whereas in a few hours, I can educate the average person to pick a suitable mutual fund and be sure that he or she has a pretty good understanding of what he or she has done.

On average, mutual funds have a history of providing a total return of about 12 percent per year. *Remember, now, that this is an average of past returns, not a guarantee.* This is a very good track record, especially considering the ease of using mutual funds, the professional management provided with them, the diversification they automatically provide, the small dollar amounts required to get into a fund, the various services they make available at no cost, such as automatic reinvestment and systematic withdrawal plans (explained below), the smaller degree of risk in good mutual funds, and the way they compare to the track records of other investments without all of these advantages.

SYSTEMATIC WITHDRAWAL PLANS IN MUTUAL FUNDS

To end the explanation of mutual funds, I want to mention that mutual funds usually offer a service called "systematic withdrawal plans," mentioned above. This is a plan whereby an investor deposits or accumulates a certain amount of money in an account, then instructs the fund to pay out a certain dollar amount each month. It is most often used by retired people or women who have been widowed or divorced and need income.

For example, an investor reaches age sixty-five, retires from thirty-five years with an employer, and receives a lump sum of one hundred fifty thousand dollars from his company pension plan (very common today). The investor puts this money into an IRA (an individual retirement account), to keep the money tax-sheltered. The IRA is invested in mutual funds (see chapter 11, Retirement Planning, for another look at this scenario). The mutual funds are instructed to pay income of one thousand dollars per month, or twelve thousand dollars per year, to this retired investor. The investor will receive this income of one thousand dollars every month. This is a systematic withdrawal plan. In this example, the income being paid out represents an 8 percent return. If this is a good fund, it should earn better than 8 percent on average, annually, so the fund should never run out of money. In fact, the investor's account could easily grow in value, in spite of the one thousand being paid out each month.

Systematic withdrawal plans are highly advantageous, especially if they are invested carefully in a diversified portfolio of several good mutual funds. Usually, you would want to have from three to ten mutual funds in any retirement portfolio.

If the funds are suitable for the investor, and if each fund is different from the others, the investor has several advantages. She will have some protection against inflation by owning one or several "growth" funds that will offer inflation protection, plus other funds designed to provide income, giving the portfolio balance.

When the portfolio of funds is chosen, the financial advisor, usually a CFP, will look at the total return for each fund in the portfolio and calculate an average for all of the funds in the total portfolio. If the portfolio earns a total return of 12 percent but initially pays out only 8 percent, the principal will grow in value. Then, in a few years, the retiree can increase his or her income by inflation and receive a larger monthly check but still preserve or grow the principal. This is a good strategy and is a primary reason why mutual funds are a good way to provide income and inflation protection.

In this age of longer and longer life expectancies for many people, the greatest fear that is usually expressed is that of outliving their money. This kind of income plan, a systematic mutual-fund withdrawal plan, based on the above concepts, protects a person from this danger. It also allows the person who wants to leave an inheritance to be able to do so.

CERTIFICATE OF DEPOSIT (CD)

A certificate of deposit (CD) is a contract between you and a bank, credit union, or savings and loan. It means that you have opened an account with them for a specified period of time, at a stated interest rate to be paid to your account, which is the certificate, at certain points during the specified time period.

A CD will pay the lowest rate of return of most investments, generally about the same rate of return that you would get on a U.S. government Treasury bill. Historically, over the last sixty-five years, this rate of return has been about 4 percent on average, even taking into consideration the double-digit interest rates we saw in the early 1980s in the United States. CDs and Treasury bills will pay about the same rate of return as inflation. So, you may surmise that even though you do not *make* much money, at least you don't *lose* money, because you keep up with inflation. *However, this is incorrect. Read on. . . .*

CDs are taxable, so, over time, they are not very profitable as investments, even if they do keep up with inflation. This is because *they end up netting you less than inflation, after you pay the taxes on them each year.* And, if you earn less than inflation on your investments, *you are losing purchasing power.*

For example, if you earn 12 percent on a CD, but inflation is 13 percent, you have already lost 1 percent. If you also have to pay taxes on that 12 percent earned, at the 28 percent tax bracket (the U.S. average), you are actually only netting a return of 9 percent. Adding the two together, you will lose 4 percent due to the combination of taxes paid and inflation.

In another example, if you earn 8 percent on a CD, and pay 28 percent tax on the earnings, you actually only get a net (after-tax) return of 5.76 percent. If inflation is 5 percent, your net (after-tax/after-inflation) return is .76 percent, about 3/4 of 1 percent. *That is not enough return to accumulate in a good investment. Good investments should earn 3 percent–6 percent over inflation and taxes combined, over 10+ year periods of time.*

So why should you have a CD at all?—because a CD is a good place to keep money for a short period of time. It is a good place to keep money that you cannot afford to lose under any circumstances. It is a good place for excess savings money. It is insured by the government, up to one hundred thousand dollars, so you will get your money back even if the bank fails. You may, however, have to wait for months to get your money, or all of it.

What about bank failures? We used to believe that during a time when many banks failed, you could get your money back from the insurance provided by the federal government, and that you should not be concerned about which banks you use. I no longer accept this as true. Today, if several banks failed at the same time, or if five or six of the big banks failed, it would put a tremendous amount of pressure on the federal deposit insurance. Today, we cannot say for sure that there would be any money with which to pay insured depositors their money in a bank failure, because the federal government does not have enough money in its own bank insurance fund to pay even 3 percent of the depositors if a lot of banks failed. The FDIC (Federal Deposit Insurance Corporation) is practically bankrupt. And the federal government is not in much better shape itself.

The United States has become a *borrower* nation, not a *lender* nation, and *our federal government simply does not have enough money in reserves of any kind to be able to bail out banks if very many of them failed.* The only thing that could be done to pay back guaranteed money to depositors would be to print more money. That is what Germany did just before Hitler came to power in Europe. Printing money to solve the problem of paying back depositors in failed banks would almost guarantee hyperinflation as well, so this is not a good solution. However, it is presently the only option available, given the condition of the federal government and the FDIC.

NATURAL RESOURCES

Too many people forget about natural resources as a category of investing and do not entirely understand what this kind of investing is all about.

Natural resources are things like farm crops, timber, gold, silver, oil, natural gas, coal, diamonds, fish caught commercially, minerals, and others.

These natural resources are usually considered renewable, to some extent. They can be "grown," "harvested," and "produced." They represent a more speculative type of investment, but they are indeed, investments. *Many a fortune has been made in oil and gas, or diamonds, or food production, just as many a fortune has been lost in these same things.*

Natural resources can be purchased, as an investment, as equity just like stock in a corporation bought as equity. You can purchase shares in companies that mine gold or diamonds, or you can become a partner in a company that drills for oil or builds apartments. In either case, you have become an owner, perhaps of just a small share, or perhaps of the total of the investments. Unless your equity in the investment is in the form of stock shares, however, you generally cannot buy and sell on short notice. This means that you do not usually have liquidity unless you own stock shares in your investments.

PARTNERSHIPS

You may be able to invest by becoming a partner in the investment you want. Business partners use this method of investing in their joint business. Often you can become a partner on a piece of real estate. If you have full liability, you are a *"general partner,"* which means that you take on all of the risk from the partnership, and can lose more than your original investment. However, you could also be a *"limited partner"* in the investment, which means that your liability is limited *only* to your original investment. If you are a general partner, you have management responsibilities and control. If you are a limited partner, you do not, as you are only a *passive* investor.

Your share of the partnership is *not* stock; you do not have shares that can be readily or easily sold. There are sometimes tax benefits to a partnership, but you do lose liquidity when you invest in this manner. This is neither good nor bad, particularly if you intend to hold this investment for a long time anyway.

It is harder and more work, however, to judge the suitability and profitability of a partnership in most cases. A partnership usually involves a new business venture of some kind, frequently involved with natural resources or real estate development. Even if previous partnerships of the same kind were successful, you are now dealing with an entirely new set of business circumstances and have little or no track record to go on to judge this current endeavor. *This does not mean that it won't work, but it does take more effort to check it out.*

ANNUITIES

There are always many people interested in "annuities." *What exactly* IS *an annuity?*

An annuity is an insurance product, a contract that you own that promises specific benefits in return for the account being established.

One kind of annuity is the "accumulation annuity." This is an account that allows you to deposit small (or large) amounts each month, or week, or biweekly into an account in your name(s).

Another kind of annuity is the "payout annuity." This is an account where you have already accumulated the amount you will deposit and wish for monthly or regular income. *This kind of annuity allows you to take a lump sum of money and turn it into income, as a pension plan would do.*

There are "fixed-rate" annuities, which pay a stated and fixed rate of interest for a specified period, such as one year or five years, and there are "variable-rate" annuities, which pay whatever rate the account earns and is guaranteed. A variable annuity is considered a security, like stocks, bonds, and mutual funds, and is *not* guaranteed.

The interest on a fixed-rate annuity pays the interest monthly, quarterly, semiannually, or annually. In addition, it generally guarantees the principal against loss, as well as the interest, but a variable annuity may or may not guarantee the principal. Therefore, a variable annuity is more risky than a fixed annuity, but it may have a higher rate of return overall as well.

Annuities usually have early withdrawal penalties, and some have what they call "deferred sales charges." This means that you may not pay any fee or load, to buy the annuity but will pay a fee or load to conceal it ahead of the term that you agreed to. Usually, the deferred sales charge is 5 percent or less, and the early withdrawal penalty is 6–7 percent in the first year and declines 1 percent per year thereafter. This means that a typical ten-year fixed annuity that has no load or fee to purchase might have a 5 percent fee charged if the contract is cancelled prior to the tenth year, or it would charge a 3 percent early withdrawal penalty if the account was closed in year five instead of allowed to continue until year eight, when the penalty would have dropped to zero percent.

Annuities are attractive, in spite of deferred sales charges and penalties, because the interest or earnings that they enjoy are tax-deferred. This means that they are not taxable until the money is withdrawn, often many years later. This means also that you do not have to declare interest earned on annuities each year when you file your income taxes unless you are actually making withdrawals from your annuity account. This is the primary advantage of annuities.

Recent tax law changes have made annuities very similar to IRAs in one important way. They are like IRAs because the withdrawals made prior to age 59½ (except for death or disability) are subject to a 10 percent IRS tax penalty. This makes annuities a true retirement investment.

One major exception to the 10 percent penalty is for an annuity that is opened with a lump sum, invested, then paid out over a time period of at least five years.

This makes annuities good investments for college funds. An example is a seventeen-year-old high school student who is given fifty thousand dollars by Grandpa for college, starting a year from now. The student opens the annuity account with the fifty thousand dollars and continues high school, graduating in June. Then the student starts college the following fall, first notifying the annuity that she wishes to take quarterly withdrawals of equal amounts over five years while in college. The annuity will make the withdrawals automatically, usually sending the money directly to the bank account of the student, from which the student pays her tuition, books, and living expenses while in school. The law does not allow the payments to be made over less than five years, however, so the student who finishes school in four years will continue to get income for the extra year following graduation from college.

Annuities are considered fairly conservative investments and are generally suitable for most older investors, and some younger ones as well. It is important, however, to discuss the financial status of the company that issues the annuity, to be sure that it is financially secure. It is not enough to rely on the B+ or A+ rating that the company might advertise, as A+ companies can and do go out of business. If an annuity company is paying a much higher rate of interest than all other annuity companies, beware. If it looks too good to be true, it probably is. Always be sure to have reasonable expectations about the interest rate you expect; in annuities it should be about 3 percent more than what you would get from a savings account.

BUSINESS INVESTMENTS

Investing in business can be as simple as starting your own business and working hard to make it profitable, or it can be a complicated venture where you get involved in a business deal with a number of other investors. The latter is often called a joint venture. Sometimes several businesses go together on a project, calling their joint efforts a joint venture. Usually, joint ventures are somewhat speculative, or will take a large amount of money to get started, and may or may not turn out to be profitable, but the investors involved feel it is worth the chance for specific reasons.

I do not usually categorize buying stock in a corporation, in a mutual fund or outright, as being in business. Being in business, from my perspective, means that you are involved in the daily management and operation of a particular business. This is definitely not what happens when you invest in a business by purchasing stock, even though you are "in business" in some respects. When you are a stockholder, you are a "passive investor," not an "active investor."

When you invest actively in business, however, you have entered into an entirely different category of investing, different from buying stocks and bonds. You will now be actively involved, usually on a daily basis, in seeing that your business does well, grows, keeps good records, markets its products and services to the public who will hopefully buy them, and pays taxes appropriately. Truthfully, not many people are suited for this kind of investment.

Consequently, I do not often recommend business as an investment category for the average person to consider. I have seen too many people invest in a business and then prove to be unsuited for business management, therefore the business fails and the investor has lost a lot of money. Read my last chapter in this book for some horror stories about being the owner of a small business or business ventures as an investment to the average person.

Nevertheless, this is a valid category of investment. It should be considered by that special individual for whom it is appropriate.

I counsel many self-employed clients and small-business owners about getting started, keeping good records, setting aside monies for taxes that are due throughout the year in a small business (not just on April 15), payroll, profit margins, employee taxes, employee benefits and pension plans, and how to structure the business so that it is the most profitable to sell eventually. I also counsel clients about the best ways to transfer this business to family members as part of an estate plan, to provide for the ongoing support of the family in the event of the premature death of the owner, or to allow the owner to retire.

Some people really *do* have a knack, probably a God-given gift, for business. These people usually do very well, but these people invariably put almost all of their investment dollars into their business. They are masters at "putting all their eggs in one basket." If it works, it usually works really well. If it fails, it fails very badly. It is considered a relatively high risk in most cases, but keep in mind that the majority of real wealth, and 80 percent of all jobs, has been created entirely by small business in America (and other democratic and developing nations). Small business is literally the "engine that runs this country" financially.

If you are seriously thinking about starting a small business, I strongly urge you to write out, in great detail, all that you hope to accomplish. This is your "starting-business plan."

Once you have committed to paper what you hope to accomplish by going into a business, you will need to write up an estimate of the costs of all of the items you will need to get started, and the prices of all of the items you will sell. Then, you will have to compare the costs of starting and the ongoing expenses that you anticipate, with the income or profits that you think you will make from this business. This is a beginning estimate of "income and expense" breakdown of this hypothetical business.

Now, you need to make two appointments; one with a certified financial planner for ideas, another with a certified public account for an opinion of the merits of this plan. Then, get a good, simple, comprehensive bookkeeping system and get started.

If you are already employed and can handle the extra load of work, begin your business *part-time. Try not to borrow money if possible,* by starting small and using profits to grow, instead of borrowing money. Build your business gradually. Nothing should be expected to grow overnight; *it takes time.*

The main reasons why 80 percent of new businesses fail is that they start out with too little cash (you have to save up what you will need, because you may not make any money during the first year) and poor bookkeeping. These are the two reasons that businesses fail. It is not that the idea was bad, not that the product was not good, and not that the public did not want what you had to sell, generally. It was because the owner did not have enough cash to operate the business and did not have a good bookkeeping system.

Don't make these classic mistakes!

THE HIGH COST OF HIGHER EDUCATION

There is no doubt about it, college costs are going up twice as fast as the rest of our expenses!

Even when inflation is low, like the 3 to 4 percent rates in effect at the time of this writing (1994), college costs are climbing by 12 percent to 15 percent per year. In the appendix are some lists of typical costs for public and private universities and colleges in the United States. You might find it helpful to review these with your child carefully. If this escalation of the costs of higher education continues unabated, college will become absolutely out of reach for middle-class Americans.

As a result, more students will have to find alternative ways to get a higher education. Some will have to delay college, or attend part-time while working full-time. Others will try to work and attend full-time, which is very difficult to do, while others will attend community colleges instead of a four-year school. Some students will borrow more money if loans are available, opting for an education instead of a house. Some will simply not attend.

Nevertheless, if you have room in your budget for it, saving and investing today for future college costs is a must if you plan to help your children with these skyrocketing costs in any way. So, if you can fit it into your budget, start today to put money aside for this goal. There are some simple steps you can take to estimate how much you will need and how much that need will take out of your current budget. Here are the steps you can follow to figure this out:

1. Decide if you want your child to attend a state university or a private college. State universities average about half of the expense,

sometimes even less, than private colleges. Find out the current tuition, books, fees, and room-board expenses at the university that most closely matches your goal for your child. I will illustrate with an example further down in this chapter, but you must use actual amounts once you determine the university of your choice.

2. Calculate how much you will need for the four years of each child's education. My charts will show you how to do this. Compare how much you will need with what you have today.

3. Determine to save and invest without paying much, if any, taxes on the money you set aside each year for this college-funding plan. There are several ways to do this, explained later in this chapter.

4. Choose an investment plan, selecting the specific investment types that you will use. Start with one or two, building to as many as ten over the years.

Let's look at the details of how each step gets done, starting with Step 1, deciding on a public or private university. Start with your child's age now. Look at chart #1 to see how much you will need, in either a public or private university. This may help you decide, and it will definitely tell you how much you will need to accumulate in either case.

These are the expenses as reported by the College Board for 1989–1990. The averages were $4,733 for a public university and $12,635 for a private university, adjusted upward at a 6 percent annual rate of inflation.

From the chart on the following page, complete the following:

List here: TOTAL NEEDED   _____
List here: TOTAL AVAILABLE TODAY _____
Difference: _____
= the amount needed to accumulate through savings and investment over the next _____ years

This is your answer to the first part of the college funding plan.

Step 2. Estimate how much you will need to save or invest to meet this goal of accumulating the amount you will need.

Look at chart #2. It shows you how much you would have to invest on a monthly basis to accumulate this amount you have determined that you will need to reach your goal. This chart works whether the goal is college funding,

THE COST OF A COLLEGE EDUCATION

CHART #1

If your child is now: (years of age)	He or she will enter college in	*Four Years at a PUBLIC COLLEGE will cost:	or at a PRIVATE COLLEGE will cost:
15	3 yrs.	$24,660	$65,831
14	4 yrs.	$26,140	$69,781
13	5 yrs.	$27,708	$73,968
12	6 yrs.	$29,371	$78,406
11	7 yrs.	$31,133	$83,111
10	8 yrs.	$33,110	$88,097
9	9 yrs.	$34,981	$93,383
8	10 yrs.	$37,080	$98,986
7	11 yrs.	$39,304	$104,925
6	12 yrs.	$41,663	$111,221
5	13 yrs.	$44,162	$117,894
4	14 yrs.	$46,812	$124,968
3	15 yrs.	$49,621	$132,466
2	16 yrs.	$52,598	$140,414
1	17 yrs.	$55,754	$148,838

*Costs are based on the average annual total education.

CHART #2

Age of Oldest Child Now	Monthly investments required to accumulate these amounts* by age 18								
	$15,000	$25,000	$36,000	$50,000	$75,000	$100,000	$125,000	$150,000	$175,000
1	$31.32	$52.20	$73.08	$104.40	$156.60	$206.80	$261.00	$313.21	$365.41
2	$35.18	$58.63	$82.08	$117.26	$175.89	$234.52	$293.14	$351.77	$410.40
3	$39.64	$66.07	$92.49	$132.13	$196.20	$264.27	$330.33	$396.40	$462.47
4	$44.84	$74.73	$104.63	$149.47	$224.20	$298.94	$373.67	$448.41	$523.14
5	$50.95	$84.92	$119.89	$169.84	$254.76	$339.68	$424.60	$509.52	$594.44
6	$58.20	$97.01	$135.61	$194.02	$291.02	$383.03	$485.04	$582.05	$679.05
7	$66.91	$111.52	$156.13	$223.04	$334.56	$446.08	$587.60	$669.12	$780.84
8	$77.51	$129.19	$180.87	$258.38	$387.57	$516.76	$645.95	$775.14	$904.33
9	$90.64	$151.07	$211.50	$302.15	$453.22	$604.29	$755.36	$906.44	$1,057.51
10	$107.25	$178.76	$260.26	$357.51	$536.27	$715.02	$893.78	$1,072.53	$1,251.29
11	$126.84	$214.73	$300.62	$492.45	$644.18	$858.91	$1,073.63	$1,288.36	$1,503.09
12	$157.88	$263.14	$368.39	$368.39	$526.28	$789.42	$1,052.65	$1,578.83	$1,841.97
13	$198.88	$331.46	$464.04	$662.92	$994.38	$1,325.84	$1,657.29	$1,968.75	$2,320.21
14	$260.78	$434.63	$608.48	$869.25	$1,303.88	$1,738.50	$2,173.13	$2,607.76	$3,042.38
15	$364.50	$607.49	$850.49	$1,1214.99	$1,822.48	$2,429.97	$3,037.47	$3,644.96	$4,252.45

*NOTE: These amounts are based on a 9% total rate of return.

Step 1.
Your child's age   _____

Step 2.
Enter the number of years until your
child begins college   _____

Step 3.
Enter the current annual cost of college,
selected from this booklet $ _____

Step 4.
Multiply this by an inflation factor
selected from Table 1   _____

Step 5.
This equals your child's future annual college costs $ _____

Step 6.
Multiply this by 2 for a two-year college
or by 4 for a four-year college   _____

Step 7.
Your child's estimated future college costs $ _____

Step 8.
Select from Table 2 the investment factor
for the investment return that you expect
to achieve after taxes   _____

Step 9.
Multiply the estimated cost in Step 7 by the investment factor in Step 8. This is the amount of money that you need to put aside regularly each year to fund your child's education. Divide this amount by 12 to obtain the monthly figure, and by 52 to obtain the weekly figure.

Yearly savings = $ _____
Monthly savings = $ _____
Weekly savings = $ _____

retirement, or any other financial goal. It is a handy reference tool that you can refer to often.

Step 3. Paying as little tax on your accumulating college fund as possible is not always easy. Congress is facing a serious budget deficit, but with a little work, you can minimize how much you contribute to the IRS to help Congress solve its own spending problems. Here are some ideas to consider:

Invest in a tax-deferred annuity. These investments were described in chapter 9. No income tax is due on the interest, dividends, or other profits earned in this kind of annuity until you begin withdrawals. Then, when you do start making withdrawals, remember that you will have to make them for at least five years (per current tax laws, 1993) to avoid a 10 percent early-withdrawal tax from the IRS.

Start taking withdrawals one year early if you have to and simply set the money aside in a savings account for your child. Have the annual withdrawals thereafter sent directly to your bank account one month before school starts so that you are ready in time for the beginning of the school year and can pay whatever school expenses are generated for each quarter or semester of school.

Can you avoid paying taxes on these withdrawals at the time that you make them?

The answer is that sometimes you can, depending on the amount of the annual withdrawals.

Under current (1994) tax laws, you are allowed to make a tax-free *gift* of up to ten thousand dollars *per year, to anyone, for any reason*. When you do

Table 1					**Table 2**			
Years to start	Inflation Factor						Inflation return, after taxes of:	
of college	4%	6%	8%	10%	Years to start of college	4%	6%	8%
1	1.04	1.06	1.08	1.10				
2	1.08	1.12	1.17	1.21	1	.981	.971	.962
3	1.12	1.19	1.26	1.33	2	.481	.471	.463
4	1.17	1.26	1.36	1.45	3	.314	.305	.296
5	1.22	1.34	1.47	1.61	4	.231	.222	.213
6	1.27	1.42	1.59	1.77	5	.181	.172	.164
7	1.32	1.50	1.71	1.95	6	.148	.139	.131
8	1.37	1.59	1.85	2.14	7	.124	.116	.108
9	1.42	1.69	2.00	2.36	8	.106	.098	.090
10	1.48	1.79	2.16	2.59	9	.093	.085	.077
11	1.54	1.90	2.33	2.85	10	.082	.074	.066
12	1.60	2.01	2.52	3.14	11	.073	.065	.058
13	1.67	2.13	2.72	3.45	12	.065	.058	.051
14	1.73	2.26	2.94	3.80	13	.059	.051	.045
15	1.80	2.40	3.17	4.18	14	.054	.046	.040
16	1.87	2.54	3.43	4.59	15	.049	.042	.035
17	1.95	2.69	3.70	5.05	16	.045	.038	.032
18	2.03	2.85	4.00	5.56	17	.041	.034	.029
					18	.038	.031	.026

this, this money is no longer yours. It is permanently *gone* from your assets and from your estate. If done properly, each time it reaches a value of ten thousand dollars, you can give away your annuity to your college-bound child, prior to starting the withdrawals. This can be done annually and is allowed *per* parent.

This means that a married couple can give away twenty thousand dollars to anybody, every year. If a married couple has enough money and has three children, they can give away twenty thousand dollars to each child (ten thouand dollars each parent) per year, or sixty thousand dollars per year. With careful planning (and endless resources) some people can accumulate and fund their children's college expenses with few or no taxes due.

ANOTHER WAY TO AVOID OR REDUCE TAXES FOR COLLEGE FUNDING

Another way to pay little or no taxes is to choose a tax-deferred investment, such as Series E savings bonds or a tax-exempt investment such as municipal bonds. In both cases you will probably get a lower rate of return, but you will not have to worry much about the investment chosen and will not have to go through the process of making gifts.

STILL ANOTHER WAY TO REDUCE/AVOID TAXES

Another method is to borrow from a pension or retirement plan. For obvious reasons, this is not my first recommendation, but people sometimes do it because they have no other money available and are willing to make sacrifices for their children, or because their circumstances are such that they will definitely not need the money in their pension or retirement plan.

USING MUTUAL FUNDS TO REDUCE/AVOID TAXES

Still another way, more subtle but very effective and probably the most sensible way to avoid or reduce taxes, is to invest in a growth mutual fund or funds.

This kind of mutual fund, described briefly in chapter 9, generally does not pay any interest and usually pays little if any in dividends. Almost all of the future value of a growth mutual fund is in its *appreciation*, which is mostly on paper, over the years.

What happens is that the fund starts out worth five dollars per share but is worth twenty-one dollars per share years later. *You* do *not pay any taxes on appreciation until you sell your shares.* So, you have delayed taxes and have more than quadrupled your value. When you withdraw money, you *will* pay taxes, but that is *not* so bad considering how well you have done overall. And, you can always use the previously mentioned "gifting" strategy to reduce or eliminate taxes if you are willing and able (assuming that tax laws allow this strategy in the future).

USING A TRUST TO REDUCE TAXES ON COLLEGE FUNDING PLANS

Finally, the most sophisticated way to reduce taxes on any accumulation is by setting up a trust. There are simple trusts already approved for exactly this purpose. They are called the "Uniform Gift to Minor's (UGM) Trust." Banks, mutual funds, and insurance companies can all set up this kind of account.

Each deposit to a UGM trust account is a *permanent and final gift to the child* named in the trust. While it sounds good in practice, it may not turn out so well if you have a child that is not responsible when he or she becomes eighteen, which is when the money in a UGM account *must* . . . I repeat, *must*, be distributed to the child. Some children have been known to take the money and run, literally. Usually this is done when the child uses the college money to buy a fast car, much to the dismay of the parents who had saved for years for an expensive college education. Even worse, I know of cases where the child took the money and partied, in some cases with friends, in other cases by spending the money on drugs. So, be careful that you know your child well if you set this kind of trust, as *it is not revocable*.

Step 4. Chose an investment. This is the easy part! Once you have gone through the first three steps, choosing an investment becomes a pretty simple task. Even so, I *strongly* advise that you get some professional help here. Do not, under any circumstances, take the advice of Aunt Milly or your brother-in-law, unless they are *competent investment professionals*.

"Competent investment professional" does not mean your banker, your CPA, your attorney, your insurance agent, or your stockbroker, and it certainly does not include your butcher or your hairdresser.

No, a competent investment professional is going to be registered as such, as a "registered investment advisor" who is registered with the state in which he or she lives and works and also with the Securities Exchange Commission in Washington, D.C. He or she should also be a certified financial planner or a chartered financial consultant. These are the professional designations that can give you good investment advice about which mutual fund to buy and when to buy it. When you see a professional for this kind of advice, be prepared to pay a fee, in order that the advice be objective and free of any conflicts of interest.

How you select an investment is the stuff of yet another book and consequently will not be covered in this book in detail. Based on the types of investments already described, however, you should be able to select the type without professional help. It only requires professional help when you start looking at the choices available to you from the 4,700 mutual funds, the four hundred asset managers, the four thousand insurance companies, and the five thousand plus listed stocks and bonds. This is where it can get a little complicated, and this is where you should beat a path to your local CFP or ChFC.

Finally, for some ideas on other ways to pay for a college education that you might *not* have considered, read on:

There are special grants, scholarships, and work-study programs available. These funding programs usually either seek a *specific* kind of student, such as a student going into a certain field of study or some specialized and unusual study area, or they seek a disadvantaged student. A list of these programs is published annually in a book that the high schools have available for students and parents to read before selecting a college.

Examples are grants and scholarships from environmental groups, nonprofit organizations, community and civic organizations, and wealthy individuals. *Look for them and see if your student fits any of the criteria they list*. If so, *apply to them all*. This way, your student has a much better chance of getting help from the Elks Clubs, the Rotary, the Sierra Club, Future Pharmacists of America, Future Farmers of America, and those kinds of groups, than if he or she simply relies on the standard and usual financial-aid grants, which are federal and much more in demand. Talk to your high school counselors about this.

Another way to fund college is to enlist in the U.S. military and get the G.I. Bill. Currently, military enlistees can get about twenty-five thousand dollars from Uncle Sam by completing their enlistment duty with one of the branches of the military. For many students, this is not a bad idea, because they can also attend college while in military service in most cases, even for sailors away at sea for periods of time, and because *many young people are truly not ready for college at age eighteen.*

There are some important advantages to doing it this way:

First, the discipline that most young people learn in the military is a valuable skill that will serve them well for their entire lives, in addition to helping pay for their college education in and out of the service. At this writing, the military in the United States is being "downsized," which results in fewer opportunities because so many military positions are being eliminated. However, we will probably always need soldiers, sailors, airmen and women, pilots, medics, instructors, officers, guardsmen, engineers, and other skilled men and women in our military forces, so the opportunities will remain even if our armed forces are reduced in numbers.

There are other government financial-aid programs as well. One is for aspiring doctors, through grants from the National Health Service. This is primarily for graduate medical school, but due to the expense of the extended education that a doctor must get, it is important to know about. Those extra years in college add up, but the costs can be almost entirely eliminated if the student agrees to work for the National Health Service upon graduation for a few years. In this program, the National Health Service pays a good salary and forgives about twenty-five thousand dollars of student loans for every year of medical service the young doctor puts in on assigned sites that are arranged by the NHS. Some of these sites are rural, where fewer doctors practice, with many in Alaska and on Native American reservations. Some are also in poorer geographic areas of the country, which means city centers as well as the rural outback.

A determined and dedicated college student will keep his or her ear to the ground always, looking for these kinds of programs all of the time. Some pop up without warning from time to time, and some have been around for many years. Too many parents overlook them entirely, thinking that their student will not qualify, before even investigating all of the possibilities.

Finally, some employers maintain an *education assistance program* for employees *and* dependents of employees. Some of these programs are low-interest-rate loans while others are outright grants and scholarships.

In addition, even when some employers do *not* offer an educational assistance program, they might know of or have access to organizations that *do. It always pays to check with an employer;* I have heard of many surprised parents who found out that their employer either had scholarships available or was willing to set up a scholarship fund right away. *Ask and ye shall receive . . . at least sometimes!*

PLANNING FOR RETIREMENT

⚜

There is NO doubt about it—retirement is *the* single biggest financial goal we all face!

Even if your needs are modest, your retirement will require more money than any other item you finance, including a house (for most people). *So, if you save and invest for nothing else, please do it for your retirement.* WHY? Because once you stop working for an income, you will have nothing to live on except what is provided by your employer, your government, your family, or *yourself*.

WHAT ABOUT SOCIAL SECURITY? Is it enough? Will you get a pension? Will you continue to receive your spouse's pension if he dies before retirement? How much will he get while you are both alive? How much will you get as his survivor?

All of these questions are important, but I have found routinely that most wives have not asked them, but if they have asked, they have forgotten the answers. This is not good stewardship to be ignorant of this most crucial source of income, especially since you will, most likely, outlive your husband by many years. Without a survivor's benefit in the Social Security income, or pension income, what will you have that you can count on for income?

FIGURE OUT YOUR RETIREMENT INCOME SOURCES NOW

What are these "retirement income sources"? They will usually begin with *Social Security* benefits.

Social Security benefits are threefold. First, they provide retirement benefits, income paid to the retired employee or his or her spouse while the employee is alive. Second, they provide disability benefits, income to the disabled employee or his family while the employee is alive. Third, they provide survivor's benefits, income to the employee's spouse or family after his death.

Let me tell you something that is really important to know. You are always entitled to either your own benefits from your own years of employment or a survivor's benefits from your husband's years of employment. Even if you are divorced, you are eligible for benefits that are based on the benefits of your spouse, as long as you were married for at least ten years. You may choose either your own benefit or a percentage of your spouse's benefit, whichever is greater. This is true whether you are married to him and he is alive, or whether you were married to him but are now divorced and he is either alive or deceased, or if you are his widow. In no case can you receive your own and a survivor's benefits.

BUT . . . you cannot start taking survivor's benefits until you are age sixty, unless you have dependents under your care, and you cannot take benefits from a living spouse until you are at least sixty-two, unless you are caring for a dependent child. If you are a young widow, with small children at home, you are entitled to "family" benefits (some of which are for your dependent children) from your husband's benefits. When those dependent children grow up, your family benefits will stop. You will not be able to resume benefits as a widow-without-dependent-children until you reach age sixty. Social Security benefits, whether your own or a widow's benefits, will be at their maximum at age sixty-five. Benefits taken at age sixty-two and sixty will be less than the full benefit that is available at age sixty-five. You *must* know this in order to be able to plan a budget in the event that you will need and be receiving Social Security.

Just how are Social Security benefits calculated? The answer is that Social Security has a formula that is rather complex, which they use to calculate your benefits as an employee or as a survivor. This formula is based on the employee's earnings over a period of years. To be eligible for benefits, an employee must have worked for at least forty "quarters" (ten years) of covered employment. The covered employment must be jobs with an employer who paid into Social Security (a few do not), along with the employee's contributions, during that ten years or longer.

For self-employed people, the payment of self-employment taxes is the same as Social Security taxes. Only a very few categories of workers can avoid Social Security taxes, so almost everyone pays in and almost everyone is eligible for benefits after ten years.

Social Security keeps track of your wages each year. These wages are entered into the formula used to come up with a wage that represents an average. Your benefits are based on this average. Today, average wages of about three thousand dollars per month will produce Social Security benefits of about $1,025 per month for a retiree at age sixty-five. The nonworking spouse of that same retiree will receive a benefit equal to 50 percent of the working spouse's benefit, or $512.50 per month, also at age sixty-five (1993 Social Security tables).

At age sixty-five, a retiring wage-earner gets 100 percent of his or her benefits. At age sixty-two, the benefits are 80 percent. At age sixty-five, a spouse not caring for a child gets a 50 percent benefit, and at age sixty-two that same spouse gets a 37.5 percent benefit. The spouse caring for a child, and the child, get a 50 percent benefit at any age, not to exceed a maximum family benefit.

Survivor benefits are a little different from retirement benefits. At age sixty-five, a survivor gets a 100 percent benefit of the deceased spouse's intended benefit. At age sixty, the survivor benefit is 71.5 percent. A spouse with one child of the deceased worker receives a 75 percent benefit, and a spouse with two children gets a 150 percent benefit. The maximum family benefit level for survivors of a deceased worker is from 150 percent to 188 percent.

Social Security allows a retiree, or a spouse or ex-spouse of a retiree, to audit that retiree's work record for Social Security account benefits upon request. There is no cost to do this audit. All you have to do is fill out a form from Social Security that asks for the worker's Social Security number and your signature. In about six weeks, you will receive a report of the earnings of that retired or retiring worker and the benefits that go with that worker's earnings. You can see for yourself what you as a spouse or ex-spouse will be entitled to.

Take note that if you find errors, such as years where Social Security reports no earnings, but you know that this is not true, you have only three years from the date of those earnings to correct the error. After three years, Social Security will not correct a report with errors, so it is important to audit your account and your spouse's account at least every three years. This could be critical in being able to get retirement benefits, or disability benefits, or survivor's benefits. To get this form, just call the local Social Security office listed in your phone book in the government section and request that they send you the "record of earnings audit form," and they will send it right out.

Pension Benefits: About 45 percent of Americans have some kind of pension. One kind is a "defined benefit pension," which promises to pay the retiree a *certain dollar amount* at retirement.

This retirement benefit is usually based on a percentage of wages, multiplied times the number of years of employment, which is then multiplied times the wage of the retiree, generally taken from an average of the last few years.

For example, a teacher has a pension that pays 2 percent of the average of the last five years of wages, times twenty-five years of employment. Let's say that the average of the last five years of wages was thirty-seven thousand dollars for the retiring teacher, and that the teacher had twenty-five years of service as a teacher. The pension will calculate out to being 2 percent of thirty-seven thousand dollars, or $740, times twenty-five years, or $18,500 per year. This is a typical "defined benefit pension formula."

Other kinds of pension are called profit-sharing plans, and they promise no specific dollar amount. Instead, they simply grow in an account on behalf of the employee and get distributed to that employee at retirement or termination of employment. Some profit-sharing plans allow the employee to contribute from his or her salary, called a "salary contribution plan," in addition to what the employer contributes. This is an *excellent* way to save for retirement.

Most plans allow an employee to contribute up to 15 percent or 20 percent, not to exceed a certain annual dollar amount, from about $9,500 in some plans and up to thirty thousand dollars in other kinds of plans, depending on the kind of plan.

I always tell an employee to contribute as much as possible to this kind of plan, for several reasons. First, it is an easy way to accumulate for retirement; and second, it is a tax-favored way to do it. This is because the amounts contributed by an employee are deducted from the wages of the employee before income taxes, making the contributions tax sheltered. For someone in the 28 percent income tax bracket, this means that for every one hundred dollars contributed to the retirement plan, twenty-eight dollars would have been paid to income taxes *but was not. It is a great way to use tax dollars to save for your retirement, and it is 100 percent legal!*

Everyone should contribute at least 10 percent of his or her salary to a retirement plan, especially if he has one available through his employment. By doing so, over the life of his employment, he is almost guaranteed a comfortable retirement from all of his working years.

Let's say that the profit-sharing plan is a 401K plan, currently a popular kind of plan. Every year, the employee puts some money into the plan, and the employer does also. Because it is invested, it grows and grows until twenty years later it is worth $175,000. Now that may seem like a lot of money, and is, but not *really* . . . not since it has to produce retirement income for a long, long time. At retirement, the retiree (or his or her heirs) can take that whole lump sum, pay taxes (and a 10 percent penalty on the money if the retiree was not yet 59 ½) or can roll it without taxes or penalty into an IRA. If the retiree dies prematurely, the heirs can do exactly the same things, then wait, let the account grow in value and take income at a later time.

There are many kinds of profit-sharing plans. Some are called "savings plans," or "investment plans," or "401K plans," or "403(b) plans" or "money purchase plans," or "retirement security plans," or "deferred compensation plans," or "457 plans," and other names, but they are all basically quite similar. All are generally based on a retirement benefit of an *undetermined amount.* Remember that the *first* kind of plan, the *defined benefit plan*, is a *predetermined amount*, while *this* kind of plan, a *defined contribution plan*, is *undetermined; that is the main difference in the two kinds of retirement plans.* I have observed that profit-sharing plans tend to grow to larger amounts of money than defined benefit pension plans, when the employee works for the same number of years at the same salary, in both plans.

Most pensions or profit-sharing plans require "vesting." This means "ownership." Usually an employee becomes *fully vested* after only a few years, typically six or seven. An employee who is zero percent vested would get nothing from his or her retirement plan at retirement or disability. An employee who is 50 percent vested would get a 50 percent benefit, or 50 percent of the amount that has been accumulated in the plan, at retirement or disability.

If you terminate your employment before retirement age and are vested to any percentage in your retirement plan, your employer must give you whatever you are entitled to when you leave your job. This is called a "distribution prior to retirement," or "premature distribution." It will be taxable UNLESS you roll it over into an IRA in your name, which *I recommend strongly that you do*. If you do *not* do this, *you will pay a heavy price in taxes and penalties*. The IRA rollover is a special kind of IRA that requires specific paperwork be done before the distribution is made from your employer to you. What is this heavy price?

First, the distribution (the entire amount) will be subject to a 10 percent penalty tax from the IRS, payable at the time of your next income tax return. You will also have to declare the amount distributed as ordinary income for that year, and pay ordinary income taxes on the entire amount distributed. For most people, that will be at least 38 percent (28 percent regular tax + 10 percent penalty tax) in total, often much more, especially with tax rates going up again (1993). *So, if you have accumulated one hundred thousand in a plan that was distributed to you without being properly "rolled over" to an IRA in your name, you would lose thirty-eight thousand dollars of it to income taxes! This is not good stewardship!*

Tax law is extremely complex, which is great for accountants but not so wonderful for ordinary people. It is also being changed constantly, with one of the most recent changes in tax law being a new (as of January 1, 1993) rule commonly called the "20 percent distribution rule." This rule requires that all retirement plan distributions made prior to retirement be subject to an automatic 20 percent withholding tax that is deducted before the distribution is made . . . IF the distribution is not rolled over to an IRA or a new retirement plan (with a new employer). This means that you must do the paperwork ahead of time, and this paperwork must specify where this is to be sent, probably the IRA you have set up. I frequently do this kind of paperwork for an employee who plans to quit, or knows he or she is going to be laid off, or is planning to retire early. In all cases, the employee and I sit down and figure out where the money from the distribution should be sent *before* the employer is notified where to send it. Then, the distribution gets properly rolled over and the *taxes are legally avoided*.

Individual Retirement Account (IRA): Congress had a moment of clarity and brilliance when it first passed the law making an IRA available to every wage earner and his or her spouse in the country. This is one of the very best ideas to come along. Americans desperately need to save and invest for retirement, and the early IRAs allowed them to do so and also get an income tax deduction, in some cases, for being thrifty and wise.

However, what Congress giveth, Congress taketh away later. IRAs are no longer tax deductible for many people. *They are still a good idea.*

IRA laws are almost exactly the same as ordinary pension and profit-sharing plan laws, but IRAs do not require the employer to participate. They are also much simpler to set up and manage. They require a trustee, which can be a mutual fund company (described in chapter 9), an insurance company, a bank, a stock and bond brokerage firm, or an independent trust company that specializes in retirement plans. A trustee will charge a few dollars each year to maintain the plan and do the paperwork in any kind of retirement plan, whether it is an IRA, a pension, or a profit-sharing plan. If you have three or more IRAs (easy to do by opening one per year), it often is less expensive and more efficient to have an independent trustee handle all of your IRAs, which can be invested in almost anything. You can and should have a number of *different* IRA investments and should *not keep all of your "IRA eggs" in one basket* of the same mutual fund, or bank account, or insurance annuity.

Your IRA can be invested in as many different investments as you want for one annual fee if you use an independent trustee. This fee runs about thirty dollars per year for most companies that do this kind of work. Most mutual funds charge little or nothing, up to ten dollars per year on average, to manage an IRA, so once you put your IRA in three or more mutual funds, you are spending the thirty dollars anyway, and you might as well get all of the funds into one account where further additions to your IRA will not increase your annual fee. I have clients with as many as twenty mutual funds in their IRAs, paying about thirty dollars per year to keep records in only one account, of all these separate funds. Instead of paying two hundred dollars per year, at ten dollars each for twenty different mutual funds, they pay only thirty dollars and they get one statement listing the values of all twenty mutual funds. Using the independent trustee is referred to as having a "self-directed IRA plan." In general, it is a good idea, one you should consider and discuss with your financial advisor. Most advisors are very comfortable with this concept and can assist you in finding a good trustee and setting up this kind of IRA for you.

In my opinion, the two-thousand-dollar annual limit on how much you can contribute to your own IRA is not enough for most people.

I believe that we will need to contribute about 10 percent per year of our annual income for about 20–25 years to accumulate enough to maintain our preretirement standard of living.

If you are contributing less than that, I estimate that you will be short of money at age sixty-five, unless you are planning to also sell a business or valuable piece of real estate at that time as well as drawing from your IRA and your Social Security. Or you may have a large pension; if so, you might not need as much accumulated in an IRA, but you will have to carefully calculate it to know for sure.

THE BOTTOM LINE: HOW MUCH WILL YOU NEED, AND HOW MUCH WILL YOU HAVE, AT RETIREMENT?

Most people will need from 67 percent to 75 percent of the amount they earned while still working. Since only about 45 percent of the population has any kind of pension or profit-sharing plan, the 55 percent without one will have to accumulate a lot more. The average pension or profit-sharing plan will supply the average worker with about 35 percent of what he or she needs to retire. Social Security will supply about 30 percent also. That leaves 35 percent that will have to come from your own pocket, from an IRA, from investments, or from personal savings.

With most of us living longer and longer, we will have to accumulate more and more. There is no way to get around it; retirement is the most important and the most expensive long-term goal any of us should have. If it isn't one of your goals, I strongly recommend you make it your first investment priority after saving for emergencies, and get started today.

ONE CAUTION: *Retirement planning is too important to leave to amateurs. It is one of the major areas of your financial life in which you should spend the time and the money to consult with a professional financial planner so that you have not calculated incorrectly and are careful and prudent about the investment decisions that you make for your retirement.*

12 ESTATE PLANNING

In this chapter, I am going to depart from the norm and do something unusual. I am going to talk to you about estate planning in simple, ordinary language that I believe anyone can understand.

This is especially unusual in the world of estate planning because of what I call "gobbledygook" so often used in the field of estate planning. It is unfortunate that planning your estate is made to sound so complicated and is explained in such incredibly complex terminology that nobody, not even professionals, truly understands what is being explained. I have tried to avoid this kind of talk in this chapter, and I hope that you finish with a greater understanding of estate planning than ever before. For, despite the gobbledygook, this IS an important subject, one you really do need to grasp and utilize. So, let's keep it simple and make this subject meaningful!

WHAT IS ESTATE PLANNING ANYWAY?

I know that you often read and hear about it in newspapers, financial magazines, seminars, and conversation, but what does "estate planning" really mean?

It simply means to have a plan that says what you want done with all of your stuff—your estate—when you die. That is your estate plan.

Obviously, if you *do* have a plan (some people do not want one, for reasons that they generally cannot explain), it is very helpful to *put your plan in writing*. Imagine what would happen if you kept your plan verbal and never wrote it down. One of two things would occur at your death: First, if no others had ever heard the plan, they would not have the *foggiest* idea of what you wanted and would only do what seemed right from their own point of view; and second, even if they had heard your plan, they might not *remember* it the way that you told it, and again, would do things the way they wanted or thought was right instead of how you had actually planned.

And, in a few cases, because the plan was not written down, relatives deliberately did something different from what was planned in spite of *knowing* that the deceased had certain wishes. This is really an unhappy event, and *it happens often*, including specific bequests and burial wishes that are ignored *because there is nothing in writing to follow*.

Do you remember the game that you played as a kid, where you sat in a circle with a bunch of other kids and the first one whispered a short story to the second, who passed it on to the third, and so on down the line to the end of the circle of kids, where it was finally told out loud to the whole group? Of course, by this time, *the story bore no resemblance to what was told by the first person to the second*. This is because things get changed in the telling and retelling. It seems to be human nature that this is so. And so it would be if your estate plan was only verbal instead of in writing. *Thus, an estate plan must be in writing in order to be useful to anyone.*

WHAT KINDS OF ESTATE PLANS ARE AVAILABLE?

There are *formal* and *informal* estate plans. For most folks, the informal plans refer to the nonfinancial details.

These plans express your concerns, *in writing,* about such things as what kind of funeral arrangements you desire, what to do with small personal items such as clothing, household items of little value, and pets that might be left behind.

Informal plans state your wishes on nonfinancial matters generally and are very useful to the survivors who have to deal with the practical, day-to-day affairs of the small details.

It is thoughtful and practical to write out your personal wishes in regard to these things. This information is separate from your will, which is your formal estate plan. This informal plan is usually kept with your will as an attachment but is not generally part of your will.

Your *formal* estate plan is another matter. It will govern how your financial affairs are settled, how your property, your investments, your assets, your financial accounts, your taxes, your debts, and your heirs are all treated. *This must be in writing,* and *it must be approved by the court because it must be a proper legal document.* Consequently, it must be in the form of a will or a trust. *It must be legal, which means that it must conform to the laws in your state.*

An example of this is that in many states you cannot disinherit your spouse or your dependent children. It is not legal to do so. In those states, your will or trust must include your spouse and minor children; it will not allow you to leave your wealth or possessions to your next-door neighbor instead of to your spouse or children. This is simply not allowed by law in most states. An exception is in states that allow a spouse to "waive" her right to inherit your estate. This is not generally the case, however, and is seldom an issue.

Most spouses DO want to inherit, and most people DO want their families to be their heirs.

Your estate plan is a written set of instructions, put simply.

In the plan document it instructs someone whom you appoint, who is called your "personal representative" (or the "executor" or "executrix"), how to pass your assets on to your heirs—who gets what, when, and under what specific conditions. *Both a will and a trust will give these instructions.*

A will is the most common form of estate-plan document, but many, many people die without writing one or getting it approved by an attorney. This is usually a mistake. Most people do need a will, even if it is only a very simple one, particularly people with small children, even if they own few assets and have little or no material wealth, because they *NEED* to name a guardian for those children in the event of their death while those children are still dependents.

Without a will that names the guardian of minor children, it will be up to a court to decide who will be the guardian, and it could end up being someone that you would hate to have raise your children. It might even be that the court would decide to appoint *someone other than your spouse as guardian of your children!*

Believe it or not, I have seen such things happen. Parents are *NOT* automatically named as guardians, especially if someone can convince the court that the surviving parent is not fit to be the guardian. *This* DOES *really happen!*

So, even if you own nothing and are poor in money but wealthy in children, you need a will to name a trusted person or persons to be the guardian of your children if you die. Married couples should name each other, of course, but what would happen if you both died at the same time, such as in a car accident or plane crash? Your will, if you had one, would say that "in the event of the death of both parents, Aunt Jane is the named guardian of little Jimmy," and so forth. Your child would be raised by someone of *your* choosing, in a way that you would approve, according to *your* values, not by strangers, according to the values of someone unknown to you, and according to the court's choices.

Naturally, if you also possess material wealth, which most Americans do in abundance (even poor Americans), your will also instructs your personal representative on how to give that wealth to your heirs.

Usually, it goes from one spouse to the other, but if your state laws allow it, you also give your wealth to others as you see fit *if* your spouse agrees and your children are grown and no longer dependent. If and when your spouse dies, and after your children are grown and successfully on their own, you can give your wealth to whomever you choose, including charities or organizations doing things that you think are worthwhile.

Or you can give your estate to your spouse and children in a trust, which is managed by someone competent to manage money, for the benefit of your spouse and children, if this would be a good idea. This is where the creative part of estate planning comes in.

DOES YOUR ESTATE HAVE TO PAY TAXES WHEN YOU DIE?

Maybe, maybe not. It will depend on where you lived at the time of your death and how large your estate was at that time.

There are two kinds of estate taxes. One is the federal tax, and the other is the state tax. The federal tax is only on estates of more than six hundred thousand dollars at this time, although there is always talk in Congress about changing that amount, sometimes to a higher amount but usually to a lesser amount. Congress would *like* to collect more taxes, and the trend *will* be to tax smaller estates, so *if any changes occur in this amount, I expect it to get worse, tax-wise.*

In any case, if your estate at your death is more than the federal limit (now six hundred thousand dollars), the amount over that limit will be taxed by the federal government.

States vary in how they tax your estate at death, but if they do tax your estate, the amount of tax charged by a state is usually applied as a "credit" against any federal taxes owed. In this way, you do not pay taxes twice on the same amount. Not that this is much consolation to the survivors who must pay the taxes!

To find out if your state *does* charge a tax at death, call your local library and ask the reference librarian, or go to the library in person to look this up. This information will usually be listed in the finance section or the tax section of the nonfiction area of your library. Check with the reference librarian for help if you need it.

If a tax is due, it will only be due on that part of your estate that is more than the limitation (six hundred thousand dollars). For example, if you live in Washington state, which has no estate tax, and your estate is worth seven hundred thousand dollars at the time of your death, the state will tax your estate nothing, but the federal government will tax your estate on one hundred thousand dollars only.

The federal tax rate on estates are very high and go all the way up to 55 percent on estates worth more than $2.5 million. This means that if your estate was worth ten million dollars at the time of your death, the federal estate tax would be 55 percent of $9,400,000! That is a LOT of money for anyone to pay on a lifetime, sometimes on the efforts of an *entire* family, of accumulation.

However, most people will never pay any federal estate tax as long as it is only due on estates of over six hundred thousand dollars, so estate taxes are of little concern to most Americans. If your estate is worth more than six hundred thousand dollars (as an individual) or $1,200,000 (as a married couple), then you *DO* need to be concerned about taxes and should definitely consult with a competent estate-planning attorney and a certified financial planner about trusts. *Why? Read on.*

WHY SHOULD SOME PEOPLE HAVE A TRUST? WHAT IS A TRUST?

People have trusts for many different reasons. Some have a trust because they are quite *wealthy* and want the tax advantages that only a trust can provide. Others are only moderately well-off or are not wealthy at all but desire a trust because it ensures *privacy* at death. Your reasons may be one or all, or none, of these.

There are basically two kinds of trusts. One is a *"testate trust,"* which takes effect only at your death. It is part of your will, because it says in your will that at your death, all or part of your estate will "go into trust," for the benefit of your heirs. *This kind of trust does not go into effect until you die and only governs what will happen to your estate at that time.* You can change this part of your will to include or exclude a trust.

There are some significant tax advantages in having a trust in your will. By working with an attorney carefully, which means to explain clearly and firmly what you want to accomplish, your will, by including a trust that will be set up at your death, can automatically place any part of your estate that would be taxed into an account called a "family or spousal trust" that will prevent that amount from being taxed.

This means that if you do have a large, taxable estate, you can set up a trust or trusts that will remove at your death that taxable part of your estate from your total estate, placing it instead into a trust for your heirs. This kind of trust is common, often used to provide income for minor children or adults who are not able to handle money or finances well.

Unfortunately, however, it is also sometimes used in cases where the heirs are quite capable and *should* have been given the right to make money and financial decisions but were not able to do so because of a trust that had been unnecessarily set up or was *unnecessarily strict*.

I believe that some people set up trusts in order to "have the last word," literally. They want to continue to control their wealth, even after their death, and sometimes this does a *tremendous* disservice to capable heirs who could have managed quite well without a trust, or an overly strict trust's being created.

Make sure that if you want a trust at your death, you are doing this for good reasons, such as tax savings, and that your heirs really will need this kind of control placed on their lives after your death. Sometimes, many times, they will not, and a trust is not necessary or advisable.

Another kind of trust, unlike the testate trust, is a *living trust. A living trust is used most often to avoid probate but sometimes also to ensure good management of a large portfolio of investments or property,* both of which are acceptable reasons to set up a living trust in most cases. A living trust is also called an "inter vivos trust," which means "during lifetime." This is because a living trust is set up and made effective while you are still alive; *it does not wait until death to become effective.*

A living trust may be "revocable," which means that it can be changed (revoked), or it can be made "irrevocable," which means it cannot ever be changed, for any reason.

As I mentioned earlier, one reason for setting up a living trust is to avoid probate.

What Is Probate Exactly?

Probate is the legal process that the court goes through that proves ownership of any asset when someone dies. This is sometimes called "proving title," as the "title" to an asset is the document that proves who owns that asset. For example, the title to your car states who the owner is on that car. If the car is paid for, you are the owner, and your name appears on the title. However, if you borrowed money from the bank to buy the car, the bank will be listed as the owner on the title, as you are not yet the owner until the car is paid for.

So, probate *"proves title"* or *ownership.* This is very important, as you cannot give your assets at your death to anyone unless you can prove that you actually owned them. So, probate proves this.

I do not personally object to probate as so many people do. I think that it is a pretty good idea, in fact, to have proof of the title on all assets that you inherit. Probate is your proof of this. This will come in handy if you inherit an asset that you later decide to sell for any reason. If you have proof of ownership, you will be able to sell it, but if you do not, you will not be able to sell it.

However, sometimes probate does take a long time, and you already have proof of ownership, including proof of title, and feel that you would like to avoid probate entirely. Or you want to keep your financial affairs completely private, away from the eyes of the court or the public (probate records are open to public examination). In these cases, a living trust would be useful.

In a living trust, you set up the trust and place all of your assets into that trust. Your attorney must do this for you, as it requires legal paperwork. Placing assets into the trust means that you change the title or the ownership of those assets. To do this, you must re-register these assets into the name of the trust, out of your own name. Once this process is completed by your attorney, you no longer own these assets; the trust owns them. If the trust is revocable (changeable), you can change this at any time, but if it is irrevocable, it cannot be changed and is permanent.

Once your assets are in the trust and you no longer own them, if you were to die, there would be no tax due because your estate would own nothing. So, this kind of trust can help large estates to avoid taxes, legally. On large estates, this is a *VERY* valuable benefit. On small estates, it is of no value as far as taxes are concerned.

In my opinion, unless your estate is very large and faces heavy taxes at your death, you have no reason to consider an irrevocable living trust. Remember, trusts cost money to set up and more money to manage every year that they are in existence, and they are unnecessary for most average people.

There are other reasons to have a living trust, however, than just the avoidance of taxes at death. Some people want and need someone to manage their money, because they are getting too old, too busy, too ill, or too unable to do it for themselves. Some people want the comfort of professional management and set up a revocable living trust, with an investment manager, to make investment decisions and give advice, choose investments, do the financial planning, and generally handle the money while the owner of the trust simply goes about his or her daily business.

Often, this revocable living trust converts to a testate trust at death, for the benefit of heirs. There is unlimited creativity available in estate planning, and trusts are the ultimate in this kind of creative planning.

A revocable living trust is useful for people who feel that they must avoid probate, although I caution against a living trust for this purpose alone. I say this because I find that in many states, the probate process is fast and inexpensive, and useful—*not* to be avoided at all costs, in many cases.

But in a few cases, it *is* an advantage to avoid probate. If this is your case, a living trust might be useful to you. Sometimes it is useful if you have real estate in more than one state, or in states other than the state in which you reside.

WHAT HAPPENS AT PROBATE TIME?

When you die, your estate will be probated unless you avoid it with a trust. The court will assemble your will, a list of your assets, and the ownership (title) to all of your assets, before passing these same assets to your heirs.

Keep in mind that assets owned jointly with your spouse, if the title has "right of survival," will go directly to your spouse, outside of probate. But assets that only say your name, or say your name and the name of your spouse but not "with right of survivorship," or as community property, are subject to title search (proof of ownership).

This is so that the courts can determine the true and correct owner before passing the assets to the heirs.

Without probate, assets that were not owned as joint right of survivorship or community property must go through the process of "proving title" or ownership. This is important, as heirs often want to sell these assets after receiving them, which they cannot do unless they own them. Probate proves ownership and as such, is useful. *It is not something to be avoided in all cases.*

Too often, a lot of public attention is given to the goal of avoiding probate, as though it were the plague when, in fact, probate can and is often very useful to the heirs in an estate situation. This is especially true when the assets are in the form of real estate; going through probate may take some time, but it is worth it if the heirs plan to sell the real estate after inheriting it. And, unless the property is probated or was in trust, there is no way to sell it.

Probate can be slow and sometimes expensive in some states. Check it out in your own state to find out the typical costs before assuming that it is the plague, to be avoided at all costs.

In some states, it is quite fast, inexpensive, and efficient. In others, it takes months and years to complete, costs huge fees, and may not even clear up all of the problems. Do not fall for the sales gimmick going around in some states that makes the pitch that you should avoid probate in all cases, and that everyone needs a living trust. Only in some states . . . and only if it actually produces some benefits for you and your heirs, should you think about a living trust.

In Summary, What Are the "Basics of Estate Planning"?

They are:

1. A will, which 99.9 percent of people should have
2. a testate trust (set up by your will at the time of your death)
3. a revocable living trust (made during your lifetime, changeable)
4. an irrevocable living trust (made during your lifetime, *un*changeable)

A testate trust is a good way to secure care and money management for dependent children or elderly parents or grandparents who are *truly* not capable of handling their affairs after your death. A revocable living trust provides you with the convenience of having your assets managed during your lifetime, safeguards continued management if you were to become disabled or incompetent, and has the advantage of being set up in such a way that it can automatically be converted to an irrevocable trust at your death.

An irrevocable living trust gives you the tax advantages of reducing the amount of taxes your estate would pay at your death by removing all or part of your assets from your control during your lifetime, placing them in the trust, of which you are merely the income beneficiary during your lifetime. It is useful on very large estates, often combined with other kinds of trusts that give the nontaxable portion of your estate to your spouse or to your family.

In estate planning, the key to remember is that things change frequently. Congress has made, and changed, tax laws as they apply to trusts, to estates, and to estate planning, as often as they go into session, which is annually. Just as soon as you have mastered one technique for reducing or avoiding estate taxes, Congress or the IRS throws you a curveball and you have to devise another. This is the job of the estate-planning attorneys and specialized financial planners. Sometimes I joke that tax law changes assure the *"full employment of attorneys, accountants, and financial planners to the year 3000"* because it almost requires the help of a professional to simply interpret these constant and baffling changes.

For you, the average consumer, keep in mind that you can and should keep it as simple as possible. That means that you may only need a will (both spouses need a separate will of their own) and proper ownership of all of your assets. You wills should name the guardian of your minor children or dependent adults (such as adult handicapped children, elderly parents, and so forth) and you should specify whether or not any of your estate will go into a trust and if so, for whose benefit, at your death.

Be careful not to place an unnecessary restriction on your heirs by setting up a trust that they will not need and cannot undo; do not attempt to control your heirs after your death by controlling the money and assets that you wish to leave to them unless they are truly incompetent, spendthrift, or incapable.

Husbands need to know that *most wives, with some education and a competent professional to provide periodic advice, are quite capable and able to handle the inheritance that will come to 80 percent of married women, without the benefit of a trust, and without the interference from family or friend*s.

All of the usual estate-planning terminology that you normally hear, such as "marital deduction," "generation-skipping trust," "lifetime exclusion," or "probate avoidance" is nothing but gibberish to the average person. It will change next year to some new terminology, new buzzwords, and new techniques. It is not useful to know, as long as you have a basic understanding of the concepts I have just presented.

You only need to avoid probate if it is going to be more costly and slow in your state than the average, or if you believe that your estate will be taxed at your death. Remember that you will not be taxed unless your estate is worth more than six hundred thousand dollars (for one spouse). Understand that trusts are useful if you have good reasons for having them, and understand that most people, especially people with children, need to write a proper will and name a guardian for their minor children or other dependents.

FINALLY . . . the following is a checklist of estate-planning details to note when doing your estate plan. Use it to make notes and to get organized *before* you go to an attorney to have a will written or a trust. I hope that you find this helpful in taking care of these responsibilities in your lifetime so that you *do not leave your loved ones to wander through the darkness of settling your estate without any help or prior notice of what is to be expected of them.*

BEFORE PREPARING YOUR CHECKLIST

One of the first things you should do in planning for your own death is to write a letter to your family. I call it "A Message to My Loved Ones." It can include friends, too, if you like, but should certainly include all of your family.

In "A Message to My Loved Ones," you can write down the little details that are important to you and not part of your will. These will be instructions on how you want to be buried or cremated, what special remembrances you desire, what you do *not* want done at your death, such as an expensive casket, a funeral with depressing music, strangers speaking about your life, or other things that people often object to. In this letter you can specify who is to get the personal items that may not be listed, per item, in your will, such as your personal letters, photos, clothing, music collection, old coins, tools, pets, and so forth. You can also leave your family and friends with your fond memories here, your thoughts of them, and your joy at having lived with them. This is your chance to finalize and cement all of those things that were left unsaid and undone during your lifetime. This is where you reveal some of your most personal thoughts if you care to. This letter has the effect of helping your family with the painful personal details that they face, and it also has the potential of giving great comfort to your loved ones at the time of your death.

Following your "Message to My Loved Ones," you will need to help them out by attaching a *completed list of all of your estate plus an itemization of where to find all of the papers.* This list follows:

ESTATE PLANNING CHECKLIST

DATE: YOUR NAME:

YOUR WILL IS LOCATED AT:

NAME & # OF PERSONAL REPRESENTATIVE:

SUCCESSOR NAME & #:

ATTORNEY NAME & #:

FINANCIAL ADVISOR NAME & #:

CLERGY NAME & #:

INSTRUCTIONS UPON DEATH:
    (whom to call, funeral home, what to do)

LOCATION OF ESTATE PAPERS & WILL OR TRUSTS:

LIST OF HEIRS: (names, phone #, relationship)

TRUSTS: (type, name of trustee, investment advisor)

REAL ESTATE OWNED: (addresses, type, title, mortgages due, bank or
    lender where mortgage or loan is owed)

BANK ACCOUNTS AT: (list banks, accounts at each, account numbers, type
    of account and title to each account)

LIFE INSURANCE POLICIES: (name of company, policy number, type of policy, name of insured, death benefit of each policy, cash value, owner, agent name & #)

INVESTMENTS OWNED: (type, title, company name, account #, phone #)

IRAs, PENSIONS, COMPANY SAVINGS PLANS: (type, name of plan, title, account #, agent, phone #)

DEEDS: (to all property owned, location of papers)

MORTGAGES: (location of papers)

MILITARY SERVICE: (branch of service, dates, rank, status, pensions earned, death benefits)

BUSINESSES: (name of business, address, phone # of key person(s), estimate of value, name of CPA, names of partners, location of business papers dealing with death of owner, instructions on what to do and whom to call)

CITIZENSHIP/VISA PAPERS: (location, whom to contact, phone #)

LIST OF ALL DEBTS: (credit cards, bank loans, personal loans, loans owed to family and friends, car loans, mortgages, loans against pensions, loans against life insurance, loans from business, loans against investments; include account # of each loan, location of loan papers, phone # of company, names of loan officers, and list of normal payments on each loan; mention if there is any credit insurance on the loan that will pay off the loan at your death)

DEBTS OWED TO YOU: (names of people or companies who owe you money, phone # of each, amount of debt, location of papers for each debt, details on each loan if no paperwork)

OTHER DOCUMENTS LIST: (location of auto titles, bank statements, investment account statements, tax returns, birth certificates, marriage certificates, divorce papers, citizenship, passport, business documents, deeds, real estate titles, employment records, Social Security records, pension records, insurance policies, military records, Veterans Administration records, and so forth)

MY WALLET: (a photocopy of the contents of your wallet, i.e., credit cards, driver's license, professional licenses, and other wallet contents that provide clues to places or people to notify in the event of your death. Note any organ donor permission given on organ donor cards or the back of a driver's license)

FUNERAL INSTRUCTIONS: *(details not in* "A Message to My Loved Ones"*)*

Update this list and your wills every couple of years.

13 Being Self-Employed Or a Small-Business Owner

❧

Have you ever thought about being your own boss? Does this sound inviting to you? *If so, you need to understand what it means to be self-employed, to be the boss, to run your own business.*

For many Americans, this is the ultimate "American dream," the ideal to be prosperous, to own your life entirely, to do the things you have always wanted to do. It sounds good to many people, and many people pin their hopes and dreams on this idea. It is *true* that most of the major fortunes in this country were created as a result of being in business, being the owner. Business, small and large, is, in fact, the driving force of capitalism, which has long fueled the American dream.

For most Americans, however, this dream is hard if not impossible to realize, and there are some good reasons for this unpleasant fact. Before you quit your present job, which you may hate, to become self-employed or start up that little business that you envision as your ticket to prosperity, *do some homework first. Start with the information in this chapter.*

CAN YOU REALLY BECOME PROSPEROUS AND INDEPENDENT BY BEING YOUR OWN BOSS? Indeed, yes, yes, yes you can!

Some people with a knack for *creativity, organization, self-motivation, marketing,* and *research,* and who have *financial savvy* and *extreme self-discipline, can and do* become quite prosperous and totally independent. This is the American dream in all of its glory!

But, this prosperous group of people comprises only about 20 percent of the total of those who try ... and fail ... in this dream. What happens to the other 80 percent? Why don't more people succeed in self-employment and small business?

The truth is that *it is more work than most people even their wildest imagination could ever imagine or dream of, to run your own business.*

It requires 80–100 hours per week for several years, on average, to just get started. That is usually because you are on a "learning curve," taking longer to do things associated with your business than it will take once you are more skilled at running a business. In addition, in the beginning you have to do everything, be the chief cook, bottle washer, janitor, secretary, order clerk, phone receptionist, salesperson, technician, and any other job required. You have to at least know how to do some of these things by *doing* them before you can hire someone else to do them, if you want to be successful.

It is also not easy to make a profit, and it is increasingly hard to find the time or know-how to complete and file all of the incredibly wasteful paperwork and government forms that every small business must file.

I have yet to figure out who, if anyone, reads all of those forms that get sent in, and if so, what on earth they actually do with all of that seemingly worthless information. Most likely, the paperwork required by our city, county, state, and federal governments simply provides someone with a job but serves very little other purpose. That is the way it seems to most small-business owners, anyway!

TO MAKE A PROFIT in any small business, you should know that you will have to charge more than you would expect for your product or service. This is because of taxes. Think of it this way: If you want to earn a dollar that you can use to buy food for your family, you will have to charge two dollars, maybe three dollars, maybe four dollars . . . maybe even more, to end up with that one dollar for your family. Had you thought about it in that way? Does this surprise you?

Why is this so, then? It is because the self-employed person or business owner pays all of the city, county, state, and federal taxes on every dollar that they take in, in various forms. They are the boss as well as the employee, so *they pay the employer taxes as well as the employee taxes.* There are *tremendous amounts of taxes*, not just income taxes, levied on every business. I will mention most of them as this chapter progresses. If you are self-employed, you *are* a business, even if the only thing you sell is a service, and even if the only person involved is yourself.

So . . . what are some of the typical taxes paid by businesses, including small business?

Here is a partial (and frightening) list:

- business and occupational (B & O) taxes, paid on gross income in some states and on net income in others states, paid to cities as well as to states
- employee taxes, including but not limited to: unemployment tax, labor and industries tax, Social Security tax, Medicare tax
- excise taxes
- property taxes
- transfer taxes
- occupational taxes
- income taxes, both federal and state (in some states)
- other miscellaneous taxes

Some types of businesses have other special taxes only for their type of business, taxes only common to certain industries or categories of work or services. All of these taxes, and others, increase the cost of doing business. They can double, triple, and quadruple the cost of earning each dollar in your business. Therefore, if they triple, you must earn three dollars to be able to keep one dollar after taxes.

On top of that, you must *also* consider the cost of your *raw materials*, your *inventory,* your employee *wages*, your employee *benefits* such as medical insurance (almost mandatory today), *retirement* plan benefits and costs (if you want to attract good employees), the business *insurance* policies you will need, your *supplies*, your *manufacturing* costs, your *distribution* costs, your *marketing* costs, your *union* costs (if applicable), your *equipment* expense, your *utilities/phone/fax/computer*, your *advertising* expense, your *training* costs, your *travel* costs, and *rent on office space*. Did you know of all of these expenses when you began to think about being the boss? *Are you still interested?*

By the time you add it all up, it can easily cost one hundred dollars or more in product or service price to net you five dollars or ten dollars of after-expenses/after-tax profit, which is what you get to keep and spend on your family or your own living needs.

If this is news, if you had not thought of it that way, it is time to do so, *now,* before your take the big step of jumping in, renting an office, buying equipment, paying for advertising, or doing anything that will cost or obligate you financially.

In my financial planning practice, I counsel many small-business owners and many self-employed people. *Most are struggling to make a profit.* Many, too many in my opinion, *are in trouble with the IRS* because of being self-employed or a small-business owner. Too often, small-business owners get started in their businesses without doing any research, and they fail to realize that they will owe a number of different kinds of taxes. Some of these taxes are owed monthly, others quarterly, and many are due annually.

Small-business owners who fail to check out all the taxes that they will owe will end up at the end of the year with a big tax bill due and no way to pay it. HAPPY NEW YEAR AND SEND IN YOUR MONEY! (All of it.)

The most common tax problems I hear about are:

- "I owe self-employment taxes and can't pay them."
- "I owe employee taxes and can't pay them."

I know of self-employed people and small-business owners who have let this go on for so long, year after year, that they now owe the IRS or the state twenty thousand dollars, fifty thousand dollars, and one hundred thousand dollars in some cases, just from these two kinds of taxes mentioned above. These overdue tax bills include penalties and interest, too, *and the IRS wants these amounts paid. They can and will shut down your business if you fail to pay taxes owed.*

So, being in business for yourself, being The Boss, is *not* all fun and glamor. It is TONS of work, TONS of taxes, TONS of paperwork, TONS of research, and TONS of risk.

WHY, THEN, WOULD ANYONE WANT TO DO IT?

Because in about 20 percent of the cases, being in business for yourself is VERY rewarding in several important and key ways.

First, you are, indeed, "your own boss." You answer only to yourself, not to a boss who can tell you what to do, how to do it, and when to do it. You make all of the decisions, whether you know the right answers or not. You hire and you fire. You approve expenditures, ads, promotions, and special sales. You work as many hours as necessary to get the job done (more than you ever worked before), you set the pace, the tone, the style, you envision and communicate the goals. You motivate others, not the reverse, and the buck stops with you. If you succeed, you are a hero. If you fail, you are a dog. You fight with the IRS, the department of labor, the bank, with your suppliers and creditors, and you listen to unhappy customers.

But just maybe, you also reap the rewards ... the better lifestyle, the excess income, the freedom to be as rich or as poor as you want, the better education for your kids, the decent home, the travel, and the security of being financially well-off. For most people, *these* are the reasons why they do it. *They like being in charge, they enjoy the challenge, they desire to control their own time, they are ambitious, they are creative, and they are risk-takers.*

If, after hearing all of the costs and problems, you are still interested, I encourage you to go for it! What do you do, then, to get started?

Here is the answer I give all of my clients who ask this question. This plan is ideal, in my opinion, though your plan may differ somewhat. If it does, just make sure that it does not differ so much that you make major mistakes by leaving out a truly critical component of the right steps to take in becoming your own boss.

HERE IS MY PLAN FOR SMALL BUSINESS: ACTION STEPS TO GET STARTED

1. *Write out the dream.* Be specific. Put into written form the business you want. Name it, describe it, say why it is unique, different, better than the competition, why it is needed, and why now is a good time for this kind of business.

2. *Do some in-depth research* on businesses like this or ones similar to yours. Go to large public libraries and read about other entrepreneurs who have succeeded doing something similar or related. Find out what they did that worked. Read all of the small-business and entrepreneur magazines in the library, regularly (like weekly). Begin to read journals that report on goods and services similar to what you plan to offer. Read the biographies and autobiographies of famous people that you admire, of people who achieved tremendous successes, of people who surmounted impossible problems, of people

with dreams; find out what they did that was key to their success. *Do your homework* so that you know as much as possible about this kind of business that you plan to get into when you do it.

3. *Write up a business plan.* This is frequently taught as a "business class" or "how-to class" at local community colleges or through the chamber of commerce. Take the class if you can find it, and learn how to write a proper business plan, then write yours. If this not possible, consider spending a little bit of serious money by hiring a business consultant who can assist you in writing up a business plan. This person will specialize in this, not just be a "consultant." Your plan will outline, step by step, what needs to happen to get your business started and operating profitably. Work with the local chamber of commerce small-business development specialists, if they are available (most cities have something like this). *Get as much help as you can before you make the big move.* Include in this plan a marketing and advertising plan.

4. Begin to put together the money you think you will need to get started. Your business plan should have calculated this amount for you. *Do not go into business without adequate capital! Too little start-up money, bad bookkeeping, and failure to pay estimated taxes are the three main reasons why new businesses fail.* Do not doom your efforts before you even get started by having too little money to work with.

Include in your capital expenses an amount of money that you will need to live on modestly (to run your home) for at least one, maybe two, years, as well as what you will need for the business itself. This means that if it will take fifteen thousand dollars to start your business and it takes two thousand dollars per month to support your family, you will need thirty-nine thousand dollars in cash before you start your business.

You should start with your own money, if possible, not borrowed money. If you have to, sell some assets before you borrow. Then, if you must borrow, start with friends and family first. Try not to borrow against your home or from the bank unless you *have to.*

If you *do* borrow from the bank, work carefully with a business consultant to present a good loan request to the banker before you apply for the loan. This reduces the risk of borrowing too much or at bad terms.

5. *Consult with an attorney and a certified public accountant (CPA) who specialize in small businesses.* Expect to pay them for their time and advice. Ask

their frank advice about how to formally structure your business (but not whether it is a sound idea, as attorneys and CPAs do not specialize in the creative "dream it up" ideas that normally get new businesses created); just find out if it is better to structure your business as a sole proprietorship, a partnership, a Sub-chapter S corporation, or a C corporation. There are distinct advantages and disadvantages to each that may apply in your situation. Ask their advice and then ask why they feel as they do, so that you genuinely understand the concepts that they explain regarding this issue. Revisit this issue in a few years to consider converting to one of the other kinds of business structures at that time.

I generally advise strongly against doing business as a partnership, even if you are going into business with someone else, as this is the most risky form of business to use, in my opinion, and is often the least beneficial as well. Partners are generally *liable, personally as well as in business, for each other,* so if you do business as a partnership, you are going to be liable for your partner's personal debts, problems, and mistakes, as well as his or her business debts, problems, and mistakes also. *This is too much risk for the beginner to take.*

When you have determined the form (structure) for your business, draw up the papers to formally set up and register your business in your state and city. You may need the help of your attorney in some cases. Get your business licenses and permits, as well as your employer identification number from the IRS (if you plan on having employees).

6. *Begin to shop for equipment and supplies.* Get competitive bids wherever you can. Consider the warehouse as well as the boutique suppliers of office equipment, computers, phones, faxes, copiers, furniture, miscellaneous small supplies, inventory, raw materials, letterhead, business cards, and signs. Do not limit your shopping to your own state; investigate catalogs and networks. Shop all levels of suppliers and brokers, because some will offer the service you very much need, the extra added key ingredient to your future success as a new business, which sometimes the discount stores and warehouses cannot supply or do not have available. Sometimes the discount stores and warehouses are where you will go later, when you already know what you are doing. Do not purchase on impulse or because you are very excited to get started; wait until you have shopped the entire market. When you do buy, purchase the best quality that you can afford.

7. Prepare an estimate of projected income and expenses for the next thirteen months, starting with the first day of business. This will tell you how much income you will need to produce to survive, to break even, to make a profit, and to make the kind of profit you must have to pay taxes as well as provide yourself with an income. After you have commenced operations as a functioning business, redo this monthly, and compare the actual results to the projected results.

Once you have done all of this, you may be ready to make the big leap. It is, indeed, a leap of faith. If you have prayed about this with each of these steps listed above, and you have searched Scripture for the principles of being in business and managing money (now you will handle *other* people's money as well as your *own*), you stand as good a chance as anyone to succeed. Just remember that the fun part is a few years down the road and just shoot for survival the first few years. If it was God's plan all along for you to be in business, chances are that you will do well as long as you are responsible with money at the same time.

Before you take the big leap of faith, however, you might consider trying something else that is often very helpful. At about step #3 above, when you start to save money to get started, you might try working for someone else who is already doing what you want to do. This is called "practicing on someone else's nickel." In this way, you learn about this kind of business inside and out, you find out and observe what works, you learn what and who will be your competition, and you understand how to actually run this kind of business. If your idea is unique and therefore no one else is doing what you plan to do, find a business that relies on the same concepts as yours even if the actual product or service is not the same, and "practice on their nickel."

The rule of thumb in this method of preparing to start your own business is to work in this way for someone else for about three to five years. It is important, however, if you do this, that the work you do is meaningful enough to actually teach you what you need to know. You can't expect to learn about running a retail specialty art gallery if you are working part-time as a receptionist; you must work your way up to being knowledgeable and valuable to the owner of the art gallery so that you are in much closer touch with the business than you would be as a receptionist. You may have to go to school nights to learn more, to impress your boss, to refine your skills and talents. Do whatever you have to do to become valuable and then learn that business until you know that you could run it on your own.

No doubt by now many of you have declared that the last thing you will ever do is go into business for yourself. If so, it is a good thing, as you have thus been spared the grief and trouble of trying something for which you are not suited. If you are still determined, however, after all of this information, you probably have what it takes to succeed. If so, you should be congratulated for having the drive and ambition to try. If you fail . . . well, you will have had the chance to try and the satisfaction of knowing that you gave it your best efforts, which is all that anyone should expect. It may work and it may not, but you will, if business ownership is for you, never wonder and never regret having tried it for yourself.

If you are one of the few persons who are suited for self-employment and small-business ownership, get going . . . get doing . . . don't put if off any longer. America NEEDS your ambition, your "chutzpah," your creativity, and the goods, services, and jobs that you will create!

I wish you the best, and my prayers are with you.